10 Common and Costly Business Killing Legal Mistakes

and

How to Avoid Them

A Business Law Bible for Entrepreneurs

By Edward R. Alexander, Jr., Esq.

10 Common and Costly Business Killing Legal Mistakes and How to Avoid Them
A Business Law Bible for Entrepreneurs

Copyright © 2010 Edward R. Alexander, Jr.

All rights reserved. No part of this book may be reproduced or transmitted in any form or by any means, electronic or mechanical, including photocopying, recording, or by any information storage and retrieval system, without permission in writing from the publisher. Requests for permission or further information should be addressed to Entrepreneurship Law Firm, P.L.

Published by Entrepreneurship Law Firm, P.L., Orlando, Florida

ISBN: 978-0-692-00770-9

For more information about Mr. Alexander and Entrepreneurship Law Firm, P.L., see pages 219 to 222.

Dedication

To Faith,

My best friend, love of my life and wife of 25 years,

and,

To Brittany and Courtney

My smart, successful and beautiful daughters.

Table of Contents

Why a Business Book About *Mistakes*? 11
  A PhD from the School of Hard Knocks. 11
  The Rules are Different Here. 12

Contract Mistakes 17
  Addressing all issues. 18
    The Effect of a Few Missing Words. 19
  Written Record. 22
  Make the other party live by the agreement. 24
    "We don't need a written contract. We've been friends for 20 years." 24
  A few other contract issues: Writing Skill, Forms and Crooks and Bad People. 26
    Writing Skills. 26
    Forms. 28
    Do You Know What Should be in There? 30
    Crooks, Liars and Cheaters. 30
  Special Contracts: Customer Credit Terms 33
  Special Contracts: Doing Business Online 36
  Negotiation Mistakes. 39
    Both parties must take something from the deal. 41
    Take time to consider acceptable alternatives BEFORE you get to the table. 41
    You have to be willing to walk away. 42
    Always go with your gut. 43

Partnership Mistakes 45
  Why have a Buy-Sell Agreement? 46
  Buyout Causes. 51
  Setting a buyout price. 52
    Contractually Agreed Value. 53
    Auction between Partners (or One Cuts, One Chooses) 55
    Specific Considerations for One Cuts, One Chooses. 57
    Formula Valuation. 60
    Professional Valuation 61
    Third Party Offer. 62
  Funding the Buyout. 63
  Structuring the Buyout. 64
    Cross Purchase. 64
    Redemption Transactions. 65
  Management and daily operation of the business. 66

> Taxes. 67
> Compensation. 68
> New Partners. 69
> Disputes and resolution. 69
> Exit strategies. 70
> Growth.. 70
> General expectations. 71

Liability and Asset Protection Mistakes 73
> How does "Limited Liability" work? 73
> The Most Common Liability Mistakes. 74
>> Entity Name. 74
>> Executing Contracts. 74
>> Insurance is a Must. 75
>> Company Asset Management. 75
>> Corporate Formalities. 76
>> Guarantees, Intentional and Accidental. 77
> Failing to Use An Easy Asset Protection and Tax Reduction Strategy. 77

Trademark Mistakes 81
> Key Trademark Knowledge. 83

Employee Mistakes 87
> Employee Handbook 87
> Non-Compete Agreements and Restrictive Covenants 90
> Key Non-Compete Information. 92

Employee Becoming Partner Mistakes 95

Franchise Buyer Mistakes 101
> SBA Research Shows Franchises Fail at a Higher Rate than Independent Businesses! 102
> The 3 Things Every Franchise MUST Provide..................... 104
>> Trademark. 105
>> Turnkey Systems. 105
>> Assistance.. 106
> You Must Read and Understand the UFOC. 106
> What's Your Franchisor Partner's Real Cut of the Action? 107
> What if the Franchisor Won't Change the Deal? 109

Business Growth Mistakes – Organic Growth 111
> How You Should be Creating Exponential Growth for Your Business 111
> The Right Customers 112
> Increasing the Dollar Amount of Each Purchase 114
> Increasing Number of Purchases 114

Business Growth Mistakes – Growth by Business Acquisition .. 117
    The Process: An Overview. 118
    The Steps to Buying a Business. 120
    Finding a Suitable Business. 120
        What type of business makes sense? 121
        How much money do you have for the purchase? 122
        How will you make contact? 123
        Working with a Business Brokers. 124
        Business Broker Legal Relationships. 125
        Dealing with the Business Broker 127
    Conducting a Preliminary Investigation 128
    Making an Offer. 130
        How much should you pay? 132
        Structuring the Deal: Asset Purchase or Stock Purchase? .. 133
        Stock Purchase. 134
        Asset Purchase. 136
        Why an Asset Sale? 139
        Liabilities. 140
        Depreciation. 141
        Why a Stock Sale? 144
    Detailed Investigation. 145
        A Lease Time Bomb. 145
        Expect Poor Financial Records. 148
        Documents to Consider Reviewing. 150
        Liens and Encumbrances. 155
    The Purchase and Sale Contract. 162
    Secure Third Party Approvals and Close. 164

Exit Planning Mistakes 165
    Improperly Pricing Your Business. 167
    Failing to Maximize Business Value. 172
        Financial Buyers. 172
        Strategic Buyers. 172
    Trying to Sell Your Business By Yourself. 175
        Confidentiality. 177
        Objectivity 179
        Taking your eye off the management ball 180
        Negotiation. 180
        Using a broker who's guilty of "sign everyone up, then bulletin board market." 182
    Letting the Buyer find the Business Skeletons in the Closet. ... 183
    Failing to do "Due Diligence" on the Buyer. 183

Appendix A: Corporation Questions and Answers 185
    Directors. 186
    Officers.. 186
    Formation.. 188
    What are the ongoing costs of a corporation? 190
    Delaware and Nevada Corporations? 190
Appendix B: Limited Liability Company Questions and Answers 193
    Is the limited liability company a new form of business?.. 194
    Members and Managers 195
    How is a LLC created? 195
    Does a LLC issue stock certificates? 196
    Can creditors easily "pierce" an LLC to hold members personally liable?.. 196
    Delaware and Nevada LLC's? 196
Appendix C: Basic Taxation of Business Entities.................... 197
    Disregarded Tax Status 197
    Pass Through Taxation.. 198
    "S" Corporation Tax Status. 198
    Entity Taxation 201
Appendix D: Business Valuation 203
    Goodwill.. 204
    Enterprise Goodwill or Owner Goodwill? 205
    Cash Flow.. 206
    Recasting Financial Statements.. 208
    Market Data Analysis. 209
    Understanding Multipliers and Return on Investment. 210
    What if there's no cash flow?... 213
    Debt Service Capability as an Indicator of Value............... 213
    Reasonable Salary.. 214
    Acquisition Loan Terms. 215
    Reasonable Down Payment. 215
    Putting it Together... 215
    Adjustments for Future Cash Requirements..................... 216
About the Author 219
How Entrepreneurship Law Firm is different from other law firms: 221

Disclaimer

This book provides information concerning the subject matter covered. It is sold with the understanding that, while Edward R. Alexander, Jr., is an attorney, neither he nor the publisher are engaged by the reader to render legal, accounting, or other professional services.

Neither the author nor the publisher shall have any liability or obligation to any person or entity for any loss, damage or liability arising by virtue of the information provided in this book.

Before taking any action on the material in this book, you should seek competent legal, accounting or other professional advice concerning your particular circumstances.

The author uses case studies to illustrate the information in this book. Except for reported cases, the case studies have been modified to remove any personal and confidential information of the parties. Any resemblance to persons, living or dead is purely coincidental and likely to result from the normal occurrence of the situations presented in daily business dealings.

Introduction

Why a Business Book About *Mistakes*?

There's no road map to building a successful business. Although many have tried to discover the simple "paint-by-the-numbers" approach to entrepreneurship, no one has found it.

With the media regularly carrying stories of entrepreneurs selling their businesses for hundreds of millions, and even billions, of dollars, one would think that building a successful business is common. It isn't.

According to at least one source, a business fails every three minutes and 96% of businesses fail within 10 years. Although those numbers seem a bit high to me, there are clearly big risks with entrepreneurial ventures.

I don't think it needs to be that way, though. In fact, I think the high failure rate is a result of most entrepreneurs not knowing just a few things that can make a huge difference. It's the 80/20 rule in effect (you know, 80% of the results coming from 20% of the efforts).

A PhD from the School of Hard Knocks.
Without the right education or advice, most entrepreneurs go through a trial and error process.

What business owner hasn't looked back on a costly mistake and thought:

"I wish I knew then, what I know now."

Although the school of hard knocks provides a great education – people usually don't make the same costly mistake twice - the tuition is usually very high. The costs from any one mistake could kill the business.

Entrepreneurship isn't taught in most high schools and colleges.

Even today, when entrepreneurship programs are being established at some college business schools, the typical entrepreneur is "middle aged" and came through college at a time when business schools taught how to be a middle manager at a large corporation.

The Rules are Different Here.

Aside from the lack of formal education, most entrepreneurs don't get on-the-job training either. Coming from a middle management job in a large business doesn't show you how to build a small business.

Small businesses and large businesses play the game by different rules. Large businesses have the ability to raise money, large management staff and access to professional advisors and their experience. Small businesses, on the other hand, have to do things without a lot of capital, the owner is typically the only real manager and the owners don't usually contact professional advisors every time they make a move.

When a former middle manager plays the entrepreneurship game using large business rules, it's like a team trying to play basketball using football rules. It just isn't successful.

Yet, when done "right," entrepreneurship offers more security than a job any day. After all, it only takes one person to fire an employee. But, what's the likelihood that all of a business' customers will stop patronizing the business at once?

The trial and error approach shouldn't be the path to entrepreneurship. That's what this book is about.

I've been lucky enough to experience entrepreneurship over the past 23 years from two unique vantage points: first inside a successful high growth technology business in both technical and marketing roles, and second, outside as a professional advisor to entrepreneurs growing technology and "low-tech" businesses. I've seen and been a part of ventures that went extremely well and some that didn't turn out as expected.

My first hand experience has shown me that the same common and costly mistakes are made by entrepreneurs over and over again, and that avoiding these mistakes can make all the difference between success and failure.

Knowing the legal mistakes entrepreneurs commonly make will enable you to avoid at least part of the trial and error approach to entrepreneurship.

I experienced this trial and error problem personally when I first started my law firm. When I was an employee of a large corporation I never had to think about collecting the amounts due from customers. It wasn't something I was ever involved with. So I assumed (naively) that people just paid their bills.

But, when my firm invoices weren't paid on time, I discovered that some people just don't pay their bills. I was 'introduced' to the process of accounts receivable collections.

While that 'introduction' hurt my cash flow and cost me time, I (with the help of others who'd been there before) figured out how to make sure that it didn't happen again. I benefited from experienced advice of others once I knew about the problem and had a way to correct it.

While the information in this book certainly can't replace experienced legal, accounting and other professional advice, it will help you identify easily avoidable problems and keep you from having to go through the trial and error approach to entrepreneurship for these legal situations.

You'll avoid having to devote time and energy to fixing problems that could easily be avoided and be able to focus on building a successful business.

Plus, because the cost to correct a problem is almost always much greater than the cost to prevent that problem, you'll save money too.

I look forward to hearing about your entrepreneurial successes.

Chapter One

Contract Mistakes

When it comes to business killing legal mistakes, contract mistakes are, in my opinion, number one on the list of those to avoid.

Poorly prepared written contracts and verbal agreements account for a large number of small business nightmares.

Here some things I've heard from business owners:

"I want the contract to be no more than 2 pages."

"The other side won't sign any contract longer than 3 pages."

"I don't understand why this has to be so complicated. This should be simple."

It's a mistake to judge any contract by its length or to limit what goes into a contract because the contract will be too long.

The length of the contract has no bearing on its purpose. And, sometimes what you want to accomplish may sound simple but actually be quite complicated.

A contract is the right length when it fulfills its purpose. It need be no longer and must be no shorter.

So, when does a contract fulfill its purpose? Or: Why have a written contract?

There are three reasons actually:

- To be sure all of the business and legal issues are fully addressed.
- To have a record of what actually was agreed upon.
- To be able to make the other party live by the agreement.

Let's take them in order.

Addressing all issues.

By far, the most important reason is the first. By making a detailed record of all of the issues we can anticipate now, we're making sure that your expectations are the same as the expectations of the other side.

I'm not talking about seeing the future. If I could do that I'd be wildly rich from trading in the stock market.

Rather, I'm talking about using the past as a guide for the future.

Business disputes arise over missed expectations. Business disputes are costly (whether or not you litigate) and take your eyes off your main purpose – making money.

Here's a simple example. Say you want me to paint your house. You tell me the color and I tell you the price is $2,500.00. You agree and we shake hands. A contract is formed (shaking not required).

The next day I show up asking for my $2,500.00. You look at the house, noting it's not painted, and retort 'you'll get paid when the job is done.'

While this may seem like an obvious issue to deal with, I've see hundreds of contracts that state how much is to be paid without saying when.

You can imagine when a deal gets more complicated what other issues must be considered before all expectations can be addressed.

Of course, merely addressing an issue is not enough. You have to make sure that <u>exactly</u> what the parties have agreed to do (or not do) is fully written in the contract. If you miss something, you don't get a second chance to get it right.

<u>The Effect of a Few Missing Words.</u>

An actual Florida court case, *Coastal Loading*, is a great example of this problem.

In 2003, Mr. and Mrs. Williamson, the owners of Coastal Loading, a roof tile loading and hauling business, put it up for sale. In early 2004, two people decided to buy the business and negotiated a contract for purchase and sale. Among other things, that contract stated that the Williamsons would agree "not to compete with the business being sold."

As often happens, the buyer and seller signed the contract before they closed the deal. So, at the closing a few months later, the Williamsons and buyers negotiated and signed a separate non-compete agreement. That agreement said the seller would not compete in the "roof tile loading" business for 5 years and would not "call on or solicit" seller's customers.

A few months later the buyers discovered that Mr. Williamson had hauled roof tiles for a Coastal Loading customer. When asked about this Mr. Williamson said the customer had called and requested his services.

The buyer was, understandably, unhappy. Eventually, the buyer filed suit to stop the Williamsons from competing. A trial court ordered the Williamsons not to engage in the roof tile hauling business and not to do business with any of the Coastal Loading customers.

The Williamsons appealed.

In Florida, non-compete agreements are enforceable only if they meet certain statutory requirements. One of those requirements is that they be in writing and signed by the person who is restricted. They must specify what activity isn't permitted.

After reading the non-compete agreement, the appeals court decided that the Williamsons did not breach it.

Instead, the court said that roof tile *hauling* and roof tile *loading* were two separate businesses. The non-compete agreement only specified that the Williamsons couldn't perform roof tile loading. The words "roof tile hauling" weren't in there. So, the Williamsons were not prohibited from roof tile hauling.

To add insult to injury, the court also decided that the word "solicit" in the non-compete agreement meant that the sellers had to actually market or sell to the Coastal Loading customers. And, because the former Coastal customer contacted Mr. Williamson directly, he didn't "solicit" them. As a result the court ruled that there was no violation of the non-compete agreement.

In other words, because the non-compete agreement did not include the word "hauling" and because it didn't say Mr. Williamson wasn't permitted to work with any of the Coastal Loading customers, he can haul tiles for any customers who call him.

The buyers paid good money for the coastal loading business and now have to deal with competition from the sellers. And the Williamsons get money from selling the business and can make more money by competing against it.

Why? All because of a few missing words in a contract.

Avoid this situation by fully addressing all issues.

Written Record.
As I said, I can't tell the future. Rather, I use the experiences of past deals and the things my client and the other side have discussed as a guide to writing up the present deal.

Invariably, though, things will come up that no one has considered.

When things are going well or normally, the contract goes in a drawer and everyone forgets about it. But, when a problem crops up, they usually break out the contract, blow off the dust and begin to read.

So, how does a contract help when a situation isn't addressed in the contract?

To understand that, it's helpful to first look at human nature.

Witnesses in court routinely recount events where one witness tells a completely different tale than another witness. At first glance it would appear that one witness had to be lying. But studies have revealed that both witnesses can believe they were being truthful – neither had an intent to deceive.

How could this be? There could only be one set of facts about an event, right?

Not when it comes to the human mind. The human mind filters memories and those memories eventually "revise" the event in the light most favorable to the person holding the memory.

In the house painting example above, I might remember that I told you the $2,500 was due before I began the work and you might remember it was due only when the work was completed. And neither of us would be lying! Instead our memories mold the facts to suit out preferred interpretation.

A written contract helps prevent this phenomenon in two ways. First, it will be clear that the parties never addressed the issue because it was not in the written contract. This is not a matter of memory – either it's there or it isn't.

Second, the written contract will give the parties the accurate understanding of where they started (because it's written). As a result, they'll be more likely to compromise or find a resolution both parties can live with. This means the relationship continues to the benefit of both parties and there isn't the time and money sucking abyss of litigation.

Make the other party live by the agreement.

Speaking of the time and money sucking abyss of litigation, whenever I mention having to sue to enforce a contract entrepreneurs will often say, "That's not an issue for me. I'm not going to sue on this contract."

While that may be true, you can't control the other side. So what if the other side sues you?

I know, they say they've never done that before and would never sue you. But can you be absolutely sure?

"We don't need a written contract. We've been friends for 20 years."

A client of mine a few years back – let's call him Phil – created a partnership with a friend– let's call him Roger. Phil and Roger were such good friends that when they met with an attorney friend of mine, Jim, who suggested that they have a written partnership agreement, they actually laughed.

Phil said "Why would we need that? Roger and I have known each other for more than 20 years. I'm putting up the money and Roger will work the business. It's simple. Let's not complicate things with a contract. Besides, that'll slow us down and make us have to pay attorney's fees."

So, no written partnership agreement was created.

Things went great. Roger knew how to work the business and bring in customers.

At the end of the year Phil asked to see the books and get his cut. Roger said he was getting things together. A month went by. Then two. Finally, after more than four months Phil got a check in the mail. The check was for the original investment plus "interest" and was marked paid-in-full.

Phil got on the phone. Roger claimed that he was repaying Phil for Phil's start-up loan to Roger. Roger said Phil was entitled to interest on the loan, but not any profits. And, Phil wasn't entitled to look at the books.

Litigation ensued and, after many tens of thousands of dollars in fees and costs, the dispute was finally resolved. And all of it could have been avoided, though, had they entered a written partnership agreement.

Money changes the way people behave, even if you've known someone a long time.

If you do have to sue, or if you get sued, a written agreement will help you win your case.

Certain provisions in the agreement can make sure that the lawsuit happens only in your home court. While this won't give you a leg up with the court, it'll certainly be cheaper than fighting on the other side's turf.

And, if drafted properly, the agreement will spell out your rights and obligations objectively – that is specifically and without flowery language. Any person with a reasonable intelligence will be able to read the contract and know what was to be done by both parties. No more "he said, she said."

Finally, with a detailed objective agreement, the other side may decide that litigation isn't worth the effort. The other attorney won't be able to play as many games in litigation (or, as I call it, throwing garbage against the wall to see what sticks – its much easier to knock out that garbage).

A few other contract issues: Writing Skill, Forms and Crooks and Bad People.

Writing Skills.

Writing a legal document is an acquired skill. It is not the same as writing prose or business writing.

When lay people write contracts they are often ambiguous, non-specific or filled with inconsistencies and repetition. For example, they use words like "top quality" or "quick" or "to customer's satisfaction." Or, they leave out key topics like intellectual property ownership, payment terms and dispute resolution methods. Worse, they very often leave out key words, as happened in the *Coastal Loading* case discussed above.

To obtain the benefits described previously, a contract must be specific, comprehensive and objective.

When someone brings me a contract they've written, asking me to review it and provide suggestions, it almost always takes more time than me drafting the agreement myself.

Why? First, the language. The contract will have terms that change, are not defined or are poorly defined.

Also, a layperson may review an agreement and think it looks fine. But what isn't there may be as important as what is.

For example, independent contractor agreements must have a clause that assigns intellectual property developed by the contractor to the engaging company. Without that clause, the independent contractor usually owns that intellectual property and can sell or license it to another person.

Without the assignment clause, you could find yourself paying to develop software, for example, that the independent contractor could sell again to your competition. Not a good result.

Writing contracts properly means covering every angle based on experience with the type of deal covered by the contract. This is an acquired skill that must be based on experience – considering what can go wrong, what are the implied expectations and the pain of past situations gone bad.

Forms.

The use of "forms" by attorneys is often mentioned with a cynical remark by clients. But forms are good for lawyers and their clients.

Over my time practicing, I've developed certain starting points for documents – known in the legal profession and by layman as forms.

It's important to distinguish what forms are – tools for experienced lawyers – from what they're not – fill in the blank pre-printed templates you'd buy at an office supply store. A good form is one that has many of the common issues of a type of deal addressed and requires customization for your deal.

A contract form is similar to a tool in the hands of a skilled craftsman.

I'm no carpenter. So, when I use a chisel fixing things around the house, the results aren't usually what I'd planned. Sometimes I remove too much wood or take away wood in the wrong place.

On the other hand, Norm from *"This Old House"* is a true master craftsman. When he uses a chisel the result is pure art.

In other words, the tool doesn't mean competence. That only comes from experience.

The use of forms by attorneys is great for clients. If attorneys had to draft agreements from scratch each time they wrote one, it would take more time, the costs would be high, the resulting agreement would not be as complete, and it would probably have mistakes. The use of forms by attorneys result in greater accuracy and a more complete contract, and they enable attorneys to focus on the key issues of the deal.

An experienced attorney using a form applies his legal skills and experience to create a good contract.

The use of forms by lay people, on the other hand, is a huge mistake. A form off the Internet or office supply store is generic or prepared for a different deal. You risk the very purposes of having a contract when you adopt a form without applying legal skills and experience to customize it to your deal.

In particular, Internet forms often come from public company filings. Public companies and small businesses are in two different worlds. Things that are important to public companies may not be important to your business and there are probably things that are key for your business that a public company isn't concerned with (and, therefore, are not in the form).

Do You Know What Should be in There?
What isn't in the contract can be as important (or, perhaps, more important) than what is in there.

For example, in an actual Florida case the buyers of a cement plant claimed that the sellers said that the plant could produce up to 250 cubic yards of cement per day. Based on the production capacity, the buyers purchase the plant.

After they took over operation, the buyers realized the maximum product capacity was only 40% of the promised amount – 100,000 cubic yards per day. The sellers refused to adjust the price so the buyers sued.

However the court ruled in favor of the sellers because the contract didn't contain any promise that the capacity of the plant was 250,000 cubic yards per day. So, there was no breach of contract if it was less then that and the buyers were not entitled to a price reduction.

Clearly when you're involved in an important deal, you want to be sure all of the key promises and statements are contained in the written contract.

Crooks, Liars and Cheaters.
All of what has been discussed so far makes a critical assumption: you're doing business with people who genuinely want to do the right thing and meet their contract obligations.

After practicing law for 16 years as I write this, I believe that most business people will meet their contract obligations - as they perceive them - if they can do so without going broke.

But, there are those who consistently leave a trail of broken promises and bad deals in their wake. Like the leopard, these crooks, liars and cheats don't change their spots; they keep doing the same things over and over again.

Of course, none of the broken deals are their fault. There's always some person, situation, circumstance or other justification that they truly believe gives them permission to break yet another contract obligation or deal.

If you do business with any of these people, you'll be the next victim. Period.

When the other party breaches your contract, you usually only have the right to file a lawsuit. Then, after spending many dollars and plenty of time if you prove your case you'll only get a judgment – a piece of paper stating that the other party owes you money. And you (not the court) then have to collect on that judgment.

An attorney writing a demand letter cannot make a breaching party adhere to their contractual obligations no matter how "tough" the letter. And, in most cases, a court can't do it either.

Having a court compel the other party to comply with her contractual obligations is called "specific performance." Your ability to ask a court to do this is limited to certain situations. And, again, you usually spend a lot of money in attorney fees and court costs to get there.

That means that a contract – even the best written contract - is not a substitute for knowing the other party and protecting yourself in every way possible. This is known as due diligence.

Of course, the amount of due diligence that should be done depends on your deal. If you're selling widgets for cash up front, little or no due diligence is required (but a contract with at least warranty terms is required).

On the other hand, going into business with someone (in other words, getting married to them economically) requires a lot of due diligence.

Going back to Phil and Roger discussed above, during the course of the litigation, Phil discovered that Roger's business dealings around town were similar to what he'd done to Phil. Phil didn't know this because they weren't business associates, just friends. Phil wasn't in the same line of business as Roger so he never heard the stories.

On a core level, if your gut is telling you something isn't right, don't ignore it. As the book *Blink* vividly shows, your gut is probably right. We make snap judgments based on perceptions and evaluation that is not part of our conscious train of thought. They're based on experience and clues and they're often right on.

The bottom line: be sure your contracts accurately reflect your agreement, that all of the things that should be there are there, and that you're not relying on a contract to protect you from someone who has no intention of following through.

Special Contracts: Customer Credit Terms

With businesses failing at a very high rate at the time I write this, many business owners are finding that their accounts receivable aren't collectible.

By the time your customer has gotten to bankruptcy court, its probably too late to do anything to get paid.

This is a serious problem especially when sales are down. When you don't get paid you have to make up your costs with a lot of additional sales.

Say your business has a net profit of 20% of sales. That means $0.80 of every dollar collected goes to pay business expenses – employee salaries, rent, etc - and, for every dollar of accounts receivable your business doesn't collect, it must collect four more dollars in additional sales just to stay even.

Of course, the easiest way to deal with the problem is not to have any accounts receivable.

Businesses should extend credit only to make additional sales.

So first make sure you actually have to give customers terms to get their business. Perhaps, requiring COD or a big deposit won't hurt sales or will only cause no-pay/slow-pay customers to stop buying.

If you have to extend credit, you could off-load collection to credit card companies. Requiring payment by credit card gets you paid and permits the customer to pay over time.

Sometimes businesses owners resist accepting credit cards due to high discount rates and fees.

Well, it is true that the fees are additional expenses. But, when compared against uncollectible accounts they can look down-right cheap. If all your sales were by credit card, would your discount fees and expenses be greater than your uncollectible accounts plus the interest you pay the bank to borrow against your receivables?

Accepting credit cards also offers two other benefits. If a customer doesn't have a credit card to use, what does that say about the customer's credit? If the credit card companies don't think they'll collect from that customer, what makes you think you will?

And you'll make more sales because customers who need to finance the purchase wouldn't buy if you didn't accept credit cards.

If you have to offer in-house terms, making sure you're not an unlucky creditor also means doing things right from the outset and throughout the customer relationship.

First is the sales mindset. In the current economic environment, a sale isn't a sale until you get paid.

Don't sell to customers that can't or won't pay you. You must learn, and keep updated regularly, the true character of your customer through credit checks (business and owner), contacting references and other relevant checks for your industry.

If your average sale is large, having your CPA review the customer's tax returns and financial statements is also helpful.

Next, your receivables must be managed actively. Diligence pays off in collecting receivables. If a customer hasn't paid on time, don't wait. Make a call the next day and get a payment promise. Confirm it in writing or e-mail.

If the customer breaks the promise, cut them off. From late payment to cut-off should be no more than 15 days. If you feel bad, remember they're messing with your livelihood.

Remember too, if you accept late payments and the customer files for bankruptcy, you could be forced to turn them over to the bankruptcy court.

Finally, make sure you're a priority. Get a signed written agreement from the customer that is guaranteed by the owner.

This isn't just the terms on your order acknowledgment which, when they conflict with the customers purchase order terms, can leave you without the protection you thought you had. Rather, this should be through a separate signed agreement that takes priority over purchase order terms and contains clauses that allow you to charge interest, collect your costs and attorney's fees if you have to go after the client and allows you to sue in your home county or city.

Again, you may never use the agreement to sue. But, just having it can make your bill a customer priority.

Special Contracts: Doing Business Online

Companies that do business online must have website terms and conditions for protection. These terms are the contract you and your online customer "agree to" when doing business.

Like most online businesses, Overstock.com uses terms and conditions for its website and online transactions.

However, in 2009 a court refused to enforce those terms. Why?

It all started when Cynthia Hines bought a vacuum cleaner from Overstock in January of 2009. After she received the vacuum, she decided she didn't want it and returned it to Overstock.

Overstock charged her a $30.00 restocking fee. When she questioned the fee, Overstock referred her to the terms and conditions.

Ms. Hines wasn't pleased. So, she brought a class action lawsuit in Brooklyn, New York against Overstock.

The Overstock terms and conditions provide, among other things, that customers waive the right to bring a class action lawsuit, are limited to arbitration for all disputes, and must have that arbitration proceeding in Salt Lake City, Utah.

So, Overstock wanted the New York court to dismiss Ms. Hines' lawsuit and to require her to arbitrate in Utah as required by the Overstock.com terms and conditions.

Pretty straight forward, right? Not so fast said the New York court.

Website terms and conditions are a contract between the customer and Overstock. They list the rights and obligations of the customer and the business.

To enter any contract requires "assent" – an agreement, expressed or implied by action, to be bound by the contract. With a contract written on paper, that assent is expressed by signing. With a website, on the other hand, that assent is expressed by taking some action – checking a box or, in some cases, just using the website.

Overstock customers are notified of the terms and conditions on the Overstock website. The home page states: "Entering this Site will constitute your acceptance of these Terms and Conditions" which, when clicked, linked to the terms and conditions.

However, the Overstock terms and conditions are below the fold and, according to Ms. Hines: "in smaller print placed between 'privacy policy' and [the] registered trademark."

Furthermore, Ms. Hines was never required to "click" or "check" a box stating she read and accepted the terms and conditions in order to buy, and the terms and conditions were never prominently displayed on the web page above the fold (the area that is visible without scrolling when a web page is loaded into a browser).

Therefore, the New York court said, Ms. Hines could not have agreed to that which she never was forced to see.

Bad news for Overstock. The fight now continues in the New York court.

What this means is that you've got to make sure that, at a minimum, a link to your website terms and conditions is clearly identified and prominently displayed on your website home page so it is visible without scrolling downward.

To be conservative though, you need to do more. If you're doing business online (selling goods or services or accepting payments), I strongly suggest you require your customers to check a box or click "I Agree" next to a link to your website terms and conditions before processing any transaction.

You're in control of making sure you don't make the same mistake (which will surely be expensive and time consuming) as Overstock.

Negotiation Mistakes

As a business lawyer, negotiation is a part of my daily activities. But for many people, negotiation can be foreign and uncomfortable. Learning a few important factors can reduce your stress and result in better negotiation outcomes.

A client and I were negotiating a business purchase a few years ago. Everyone sat at a large conference table for many hours discussing terms and contracts.

At one point the seller got mad. He wanted my client to accept his contract provisions as is and close the deal. When we refused the take-it-or-leave-it offer, he threw his chair back and stormed out of the room.

My client was confused and worried. Had he lost the business? Should he capitulate?

I suggested that we get up and leave immediately and we started walking out.

My client couldn't lose unless he stayed. Either the seller would come get us and we'd have more leverage, or the deal was over. But, no more harm would be done by leaving.

Just as we left the office, the seller's attorney came running out the door saying she'd "calmed her client." We went back to the table, only with more leverage. The seller's outburst backfired because it was a ploy and he wasn't willing to let the deal die.

This shows how a simple mistake can harm your negotiating strength.

Negotiating from a position of strength requires that you focus on a few key factors.

Both parties must take something from the deal.

One sided deals rarely stick. The "losing" party finds a way to undo the deal or doesn't follow through. When that happens, the "winning" party loses too.

This means you must consider the goals and objectives of the other side and how you (yes you) can achieve them.

Inexperienced negotiators usually think of a one variable zero sum arrangement – I only win if you lose. They focus only on price or money.

But, there are many other variables to a negotiation. Some are of great importance to one side and of no importance to the other. So dig below the surface to see various options.

Take time to consider acceptable alternatives BEFORE you get to the table.

Doing this at the negotiating table is a sure ticket to a bad deal.

Break your requirements into best case and minimum acceptable deals. The minimum acceptable deal is the point below which you will not go, no matter what.

Of course, this requires an understanding of the risks and benefits of various approaches. Otherwise you don't know what you're giving or getting. You've got to get help and input here.

Planning your approach without the help of an experienced advisor who is only on your side is like buying a used car without having a mechanic do a full inspection. People do it all the time. Some of them get away with it. Most have problems.

Make a pact with yourself today that you won't do a deal below the minimum acceptable level. We humans are great at rationalizing. And, the light of day can reveal the harsh reality of an ill conceived arrangement at the negotiating table.

To know where that is, consider your alternatives to a negotiated arrangement. Is there another business or home you could purchase? What costs, losses and benefits are there if you don't do a deal?

By the way, you might be wrong. In fact, you could be far from where the other side is willing to go. This, of course, leads to the next point:

<u>You have to be willing to walk away.</u>
A big mistake I see quite often is "falling in love" or a "must have" deal. This means you have to have the business, house, car, or deal, no matter what. If you fall in love with it, you lose all negotiating strength because you won't (or can't) say 'no.'

There is always – and I mean always – another deal. Just because this seller is unreasonable doesn't mean you have to be the one to capitulate. Don't do it. You'll surely regret it later.

There is a great deal of power in "walking away," when its done right. As my client's story shows, if you walk away and come crawling back, you'll lose negotiating strength. You must be willing to stick with it and you can only walk away once or, maybe, twice. Brinksmanship can only be used sparingly.

Of course, you don't have to be dramatic. You can merely state that you can't do the deal unless the issue is resolved in the manner you favor.

Always go with your gut.
If you feel uncomfortable, there's usually a good reason.

When the other side makes a take-it-or-leave-it-now offer, I've found its best to say no. My usual response is: "I have to think about it. But, if you need an answer now, then the answer no."

If you consider each of these factors, you will negotiate from a position of strength and avoid being on the losing end of any deal.

Chapter Two

Partnership Mistakes

Partner[1] mistakes account for many business failures and lots of sleepless entrepreneurial nights.

Here's a situation I see all the time:

> "When my partner and I started this business, we'd been friends for 10 years. I trusted him and he trusted me. We didn't need an agreement between us. We just did the right thing.
>
> Things have changed. Now, he's only in it for himself. I do all the work and he's taking more than his share. What can I do?"

Some would assume the mistake was having a partner in the first place.

But that's not right

---

[1] Although the term "Partner" is used in this chapter, it is used in the generic definition and <u>NOT</u> the legal definition.

Well thought out and documented partnerships can propel a business to much higher levels of growth and performance than a solo partner.

No, the real partnership mistakes are:

- Not properly discussing the goals, roles, and expectation of each partner
And
- Not having a written agreement that reflects that discussion and the particulars of your business.

Why have a Buy-Sell Agreement?[2]

A business partnership is an economic marriage that, like a marriage, takes work. The written agreement helps the economic marriage work because it sets a "default" to be used when the partners can't agree.

Plus partnerships aren't for life. There will be a time when you or your partner will leave the business. It might be horizontally (on a stretcher) or vertically (walking out the

---

[2] Partnership Agreements go by many different names: shareholders agreement, buy-sell agreement, operating agreement, management agreement, etc. To make things easy, in this section I'm referring to: all partnership agreements, whether for a corporation, an LLC or legal partnership, as "shareholders agreements"; all owners, whether shareholders, members, or partners; and all ownership interests, whether shares, membership interests, or partnership interest as "shares". You can convert the terminology to the entity you use in your business.

door). But, like death and taxes, you can be certain you will leave your business.

Of course, getting all of the partners' expectations in writing makes for a better and longer term partnership.

In my opinion, though, dealing with partners who leave is the most important reason to have a shareholders agreement. Business divorces – breakups between partners – can be messy, costly and time consuming. They can also kill your successful business.

To avoid a messy business divorce and protect your business, you must have a shareholders agreement in place long before any problem comes up. If you wait until the business is "successful," it's probably too late.

Why? Because the partners interests' will change.

At the beginning of the venture it's all an unknown with lots of possibilities. But what happens when something changes. What if one partner becomes ill? Or, one gets a divorce. Or another personal circumstance changes.

In the event of a partner's sickness, the healthy partner might want to increase his salary and reduce profits distributions meaning the healthy partner would take home more of the net. Maybe that is right. Maybe not. But the time to decide is before things change.

Also, if a partner becomes terminally or chronically ill, that partner might be uninsurable, substantially complicating the buy-sell agreement and funding a buyout.

So don't make the mistake of waiting to do a shareholders agreement. Get one in place when you start the business.

Shareholders agreements come in a variety of sizes and shapes.

Unfortunately, most of them don't work.

Why? Instead of providing a fair and orderly method for a partner to leave, the shareholders agreement doesn't permit anyone to leave at all, making an already bad situation worse.

The standard "off the shelf" shareholders agreement permits a partner to sell her stock to an outsider only after offering it to the other partner at the same price. In theory a "fair price" is then set by the market.

What is usually missing, though is the outside buyer.

The reality is: Who in their right mind would buy part of a small business, especially one where the partners are fighting?

Think about that if you were the outside buyer. Before you'd buy any business where you'd have a partner, you'd want to make sure you knew the partner well and the partner was honest and competent. Plus, as a minority shareholder you'd rightly want some control or agreement in place that protected you. Buying without those things would be a gamble. Therefore, you'd only pay a small fraction of the value of the stock. You'd probably not buy at all

Yet, if there was an adequate shareholders agreement, the partners would not need the outside buyer because the agreement would provide a method to resolve the dispute.

So, in reality there are no outside offers to set a value and the already unhappy partners can't agree on a withdrawal price. The one leaving thinks the business is a gold mine, and the one remaining thinks it's about to fail

No one can leave and no one can stay. So what happens?

In the end the business leaves instead of the partners! Because most businesses required the daily interaction and work of the partners, the dispute between the partners wrecks the business. Soon nothing is left and all the value and equity is lost. The partners are on to new businesses or, worse, left holding the bag for business debts they've guaranteed.

The important thing to know to avoid that scenario is that a shareholders agreement is not "one size fits all." (You know the kind: straight from the Internet or a fill in the blank form bought at an office supply store.) Because you, your partner and your business are unique, your shareholders agreement must be tailored to your business and your goals.

Other reasons to have a shareholders agreement include:

- It protects the surviving shareholder if one dies. Do you want to be in business with your partner's spouse, or worse, his children?

   Another professional I know recently told me about a business partner who thought he had a shareholders agreement because he and his partner verbally agreed to buy each others wives out of the business upon death. The shareholders agreement <u>must</u> be in writing to ensure this happens.

- It makes sure you know who you're in business with. The shareholders agreement will allow you to prevent your partner from transferring her stock without you being able to approve the purchaser. Would you go into business with just any stranger off the street?

- It protects you from "K-1 Revenge." K-1 Revenge is a nasty way for majority partners to stick you with a tax liability for business profits <u>without</u> giving you any cash to pay that tax.

- It gives the partners an orderly predictable way to retire from the business and realize the value and wealth they've created in the business.
- It can set each partner's responsibilities and positions and avoid the situation of one partner living off the efforts of the other.
- It can help avoid a deadlock in management or the business.
- It can ensure a majority partner (or partners) can't treat the business as his own personal slush fund, drain that business bank accounts and use the assets for his personal benefit.

The following are some of the more important issues to consider when preparing your shareholders agreement.

Buyout Causes.

The causes for a partner to leave a business fall into two categories: voluntary and involuntary.

Involuntary causes include death, disability or the involuntary transfer of a partner's shares as a result of divorce or creditor claims (the creditor took control of the shareholder's stock).

Voluntary causes mean the partner retired or decided to pursue some other dream or vocation, the partner got an offer from an outside buyer he couldn't refuse, or the partners are in a dispute (i.e., a business divorce).

Whether the reason for the transfer is voluntary or involuntary will determine the method to establish the buyout price, how the purchase is funded and paid and other terms and conditions of the buyout.

Setting a buyout price.

The value of a partner's shares is determined by first valuing the "enterprise" – the going concern, business owned by the corporation. That value is then adjusted pro-rata for the partnership interest of the departing partner and, if that partner holds less than a majority interest, possibly applying a minority discount.

Until a willing buyer and a willing seller agree and complete a business sale, determining the value of any business is an educated estimate. Sometimes that guess is educated and based on facts and objective criteria, and other times it is based purely on emotion (e.g., *'this is my baby and I'm not letting it go for anything less than $5MM'*).

There are five ways to establish the value of your business for purposes of a buy-sell agreement:

1. Setting a contractually agreed value.
2. An auction between partners also known as 'one cuts, one chooses.'
3. A formula based on the financial results or other business metrics.
4. Business valuation by a qualified business appraiser or business broker.
5. A third party offer.

The methods above are ordered in increasing cost or time, and reliability (i.e., option one being the least expensive, least time consuming and the least reliable).

Contractually Agreed Value.

This method can be used for both voluntary and involuntary transfers. With this method the partners agree to a specific value for the business and update that value on a regular basis, typically once a year.

There are two serious problems with this method. First, in 16 years practicing law I've never seen a situation where the partners actually update the value regularly. When they don't, the first partner to die (and his / her family) usually loses.

Jim and Mary (not married) started a vending machine business in 1992. In 1993, Jim's financial advisor convinced them that a buy-sell agreement was a good idea. But, Jim didn't want to pay an attorney to draft the agreement. So, he got one from the Internet. That agreement valued the business through a "Certificate of Value" that the partners were to update annually.

As is typically the case, the updated it once, in 1995, when they "believed" the business was worth $100,000.00.

In 2004 Mary was diagnosed with cancer. In 2006 Mary died. At that time the net profit of the business was in excess of $600,000 and Mary's shares were conservatively estimated to be worth $720,000.00.

But, because they hadn't updated the shareholders agreement since 1995, Jim bought Mary's stock from her children (heirs) for $50,000.00 – half the agreed value of $100,000.00.

Mary unintentionally gave Jim a $670,000 gift.

The Jim - Mary situation also highlights the second problem with a contractually agreed value. What would have happened had Mary and Jim actually sat down to reset the contractually agreed value in 2005 after Mary had been diagnosed with cancer?

Knowing that the circumstances had changed, Jim might have artificially depressed his view of the value of the business. He might have refused to update the value at all. In either case the value would have been essentially stuck at the 2004 amount and, again, the first to die, Mary, and her family lose.

One way to deal with this problem is to set a time limit on the certificate of value. This would typically be 12 to, at most, 24 months. Then, if the certificate expires, the enterprise value is determined by one of the other methods.

A final problem with this method is that the partners of a business rarely have a true sense of its value. Chapter Ten discusses this further.

Auction between Partners (or One Cuts, One Chooses).

This method works only for voluntary transfers. I call it: One Cuts, One Chooses.

I have two daughters. When they were young and both wanted the last piece of cake we had a custom for resolving the dispute. One of my daughters would be allowed to cut the cake "in half." Then, the other daughter would get to choose first which half of the cake she wants to eat. I can assure you that when this happened the daughter making the cut was as precise in finding the halfway point as a brain surgeon in the operating room.

This same arrangement can be used in a shareholders agreement.

A partner wanting to initiate the breakup of the partnership would make an offer to the other partner to buy the other partner's shares. That offer would contain detailed information about price and terms and be presented, in writing, to that other partner.

Then that other partner would have a limited period of time to consider two (and only two) alternatives:
1.) accept the offer and sell his shares to the initiating partner; or
2.) turn the offer around and buy the initiating partner's shares on the terms and conditions described in the initiating partner's offer.

'One Cuts, One Chooses' works well because each partner has to be reasonable. The initiating partner has to make an offer that she is willing to accept herself.

Plus, the initiating partner can make an offer that will likely result in the outcome she wants. If she wants the other partner to buy her out, the initiating offer she makes can be at a discount to the real value. On the other hand, if she believes the business will exceed expectations, she can offer to pay a premium for her partner's shares.

Also, no partner can cause financial stress for the business that they wouldn't be able to endure themselves. If a voluntary buyout is based on a formula or valuation and one partner can trigger the buyout, the remaining partner is put at a disadvantage because business cash flow is diverted from the operation of the business and dividends to partners, to paying the departing partner.

That said, 'One Cuts, One Chooses' doesn't work well when one of the partners is at a financial disadvantage.

If the initiating partner knows the other does not have access to cash or the ability to secure a loan, the initiating partner can make a low-ball all cash offer to the other partner and that other partner, because he can't get the money to flip the deal on the initiating partner, must then sell to the initiating partner at the low-ball price.

Specific Considerations for One Cuts, One Chooses.

A recent Florida court decision about a 'One Cuts, One Chooses' provision highlights why all parts of the shareholders agreement must work together in this situation.

Protecting Business Value in a Partner Disagreement Buy Out.

Of course, for a 'One Cuts, One Chooses' process to work, there has to be some value in the business after the buy-out.

For most businesses, the primary value comes from cash flow arising from customer relationships, also known as "goodwill".

To get a clear view of this value, consider this question: Would you buy a business if you knew the seller could set up shop a block from you a week after the sale, then call your newly purchased customers to get them to switch to his new shop? Of course you wouldn't.

And no one buying out his partner wants that to happen to him either.

So, to preserve the business value and the business goodwill, the shareholders agreement should also include restrictive covenants (non-compete, non-solicitation and non-disclosure). Those restrictive covenants prohibit the partners from competing with the business while they are shareholders as well as after being bought out.

So what happens if the initiating partner in a 'One Cuts, One Chooses' process offers to buyout his partner for an absurdly low price, but <u>only</u> if there is also a termination of the non-compete portion of the partnership agreement?

Say your business is worth $1,000,000 and you're the "inside" partner. You run the back office operations of the business, controlling production and managing the finances.

Your partner, on the other hand, is the sales guy. He's out of the office selling to get new business. The customers know him as the face of the company.

One day the sales partner decides he no longer needs you. He thinks he can hire a manager to do your job and keep for himself the difference between the manager's salary and your half of the profits. So, sales partner invokes the 'One Cuts, One Chooses' provision of your buy-sell agreement and makes an offer to buy your 50% interest in the business for $10,000, an incredibly low offer, with one of the condition: the non-compete portion of the buy-sell is to be terminated.

You're faced with a lose-lose arrangement, either selling your interest to him for $10,000 or buying his interest for $10,000.

You certainly don't want to give away $500,000 of stock for $10,000.

Yet, you know that after you buy his interest according to the terms of the offer, he won't be bound by a non-compete. The next day he'll be soliciting your customers. And, because he's the face of your company, those customers will surely go with him, rendering the company you just bought worthless.

Not good for you.

Well, something similar happened in a Florida case known as *P&O Ports Florida*. There the 'Chooser' partner filed suit to declare the offer invalid.

The 'Chooser' partner was successful in the case and the waiver of the restrictive covenants as a condition to the purchase was held by the court to be invalid. But, there are a couple of mistakes made in that shareholders agreement that you'll want to avoid.

First, the court determined the shareholder agreement language was "ambiguous" – a very bad thing when it comes to negotiated contracts. This means the court decided that it should, after hearing testimony, determine what the parties "really" meant.

Of course, what the parties actually meant when they wrote the shareholders agreement is much different than what they believe they meant today.

Most entrepreneurs want to decide what the contract means when it's written, rather than letting a judge, who has no experience with you, your partner or your business, decide that as part of a lawsuit. In fact, the whole point of a contract is to make sure you know, up-front, what is going to happen without having to go to court and without having to spend tens of thousands of dollars on attorneys' fees.

What this case means for your shareholders agreement is that, in addition to 'One Cuts, One Chooses' and restrictive covenants provisions, in your shareholders agreement must also state that terminating the non-compete (or non-solicitation or non-disclosure) cannot be a part of 'One Cuts, One Chooses' offer. Otherwise, there might be nothing worth buying.

One other thing came out of this case for your shareholders agreement. During the case the initiating partner tried to rescind the offer. This caused one of the judges to believe it should have been closed. But, had the court not finally decided the case, the issue would've remained unresolved (even after the owners spent all that time and money). It would surely have come up again later in the relationship.

Letting a partner take back 'One Cuts, One Chooses' offer is like trying to put the pieces of the cake back together. It makes the whole process unfair because the initiating partner gets to "test the waters" before truly committing to an offer. He can see which way the other partner will go without having to live by the offer. So the entire fairness mechanism is lost.

Formula Valuation.

Another method that is better than a certificate of value, is to set a buyout price based on a formula using the business' operations or financial information.

This method works for both voluntary and involuntary transfers. For example, a health club business might be worth $500 multiplied by the number of members. Or, it could be 3 times the net profit or EBITDA* after adding back certain partner benefits such as company cars or club memberships, etc.

The benefit of a formula is simplicity. All the partners have to do is plug the current financial data into the formula to get the buyout price. Plus the value is tied to actual results, making it realistic.

The problem with a formula is that it doesn't change when the business model changes. So, if we are membership focused today, but the business changes and a better valuation would be based on net earnings, the formula is set and all partners have to be willing to change the agreement, to revise the formula. For the reasons described in the section discussing certificates of value, this could be problematic.

Professional Valuation

Still better and more accurate, as well as, the most expensive method to set the buyout price is a business valuation. A third party qualified business appraiser analyzes the business to determine a range of values with the median value being used for the buyout price. Business valuation is discussed in detail in Appendix D.

---

*Earnings Before Interest, Taxes Deprecation and Amortization, a financial metric of business that is approximately the same as operating cash flow of that business

Third Party Offer.

Finally, because actual value (rather than a good estimate) can only be determined once a wiling buyer and a willing seller, each with all of the information they should have, agree on a price and complete a deal, the most accurate means to establish value is a third party offer.

Of course, this only works for voluntary transfers and, as discussed at the beginning of this chapter, third party offers are few in coming. In the case of a bona fide third-party offer, the shareholder's agreement will typically require the partners who intend to accept the offer to let the other partners buy her out on the terms of the third-party offer (a right of first refusal). Therefore, terms and conditions of the purchase (e.g., cash or note, etc.) are set by the third party offer.

If the terms are not those from the offer, then the arrangement is flawed and not truly a third party offer.

The way it should work is that the other partners review the third party offer. If they believe it to be a good offer or they don't want the proposed purchaser to become a partner, they can purchase the interest of the departing partner. Otherwise, they can let the third party buy in and become a partner.

Given the right of first refusal, it's important to limit who can make an offer. You may want to exclude competitors and other unacceptable parties from buying in under any circumstances.

Funding the Buyout.
Funding a buyout will either come from insurance proceeds or business cash flow.

For a buyout of a deceased partner, it is crucial for the continued viability of the business and the deceased partner's heirs that the funding be provided through life insurance. Without the proceeds from an insurance policy, the likelihood that the buyout will be completed is seriously reduced. The surviving partners, no matter how much good faith they have, will eventually tire of working to generate cash to pay their deceased partner's heirs.

Furthermore, if the deceased partner was active in the business, proceeds from the policy can help to minimize the loss caused by the partner's death. This can help smooth the tough time when the partner's employment duties must be replaced and keep the business afloat.

For voluntary buyouts, the funding is typically the cash flow from the business operations or the profits allocated to the partners. First, there isn't usually an insurance option for these buyouts. Second, if payments stop, the partner receiving payments could conceivably take over the business.

Structuring the Buyout.

Who receives the money from the life insurance policy and how the purchase is completed can have big tax effects.

There are two basic methods for completing a buyout: cross purchase and redemption.

Cross Purchase.

In a cross purchase transaction, the buying partner (or partners) buys the stock of the selling or deceased partner and the life insurance policy on each partner is owned by the other partner (or partners). For example, if Dan and Lori are partners of Doomed, Inc., Dan would own a life insurance policy on the life of Lori and Lori on the life of Dan.

So, if Dan dies, Lori receives the money from the insurance policy and pays that money to Dan's heirs in exchange for Dan's stock. She'll then own all of the stock of Doomed, Inc.

If there is more than one partner, then each partner receives a pro rata portion of the insurance proceeds and buys a pro rata amount of the stock of the deceased partner.

The benefit of this structure is that the buying partner almost always receives the life insurance proceeds tax free. Then, when she uses the proceeds to buy the deceased partner's stock, she gets a cost basis in that stock in the amount of the purchase price.

So, when the business is ultimately sold, she doesn't pay tax on that cost basis – essentially receiving that money tax free.

For example, if Dan's insurance policy was for $100,000 and on his death Lori used that to buy Dan's stock, it is treated as though Lori personally paid $100,000.00 for that stock.

The life insurance proceeds can also be increased to cover the drop in business income that could come about as a result from Dan's death. By having these proceeds in the hands of Lori, she can determine how best to use them and, they're not at risk to claims of the company's creditors.

Of course, Dan has to make sure to secure his claim to the insurance proceeds through a collateral assignment of proceeds from the policy on his life, that is owned by Lori. That will protect that money from the claims of Lori's creditors. Dan will want to be sure that his heirs get that money, not Lori's creditors.

Redemption Transactions.

In a redemption transaction, the corporation buys the stock of the selling or deceased partner and the life insurance on the partners is owned by the corporation.

Using Dan, Lori and Doomed, Inc., again, the life insurance policy on Dan's life is owned by Doomed, Inc. When Dan dies, the insurance company pays Doomed, Inc., which buys Dan's stock from his heirs.

This scenario works well when there are many partners and it isn't feasible to set up a cross purchase with many partners owning one policy. However, care must be exercised when structuring a redemption arrangement to be sure that, when life insurance proceeds are paid, they're not treated as taxable income to the corporation. You don't want the IRS to get a cut of the policy proceeds.

Similarly, the proceeds could be subject to the claims of creditors of the corporation. So, it's important to have a collateral assignment of the proceeds as described previously.

Finally, as described below, the remaining partners don't get the tax benefit of the increase in "basis" described in the cross purchase section above. That means when Lori sells Doomed, Inc., she will have to pay taxes on the $100,000 from the insurance policy that was used to buy Dan's stock.

Management and daily operation of the business.
Are all of the partners "hands-on" people or would they rather play a more passive role? If one is hands-on and the other isn't, this should be reflected in roles and salary.

Who will be the one person in charge of the business? Multiple partners claiming to be in charge will only confuse employees and the market. While partners can exercise control through a board of directors, there has to be one chief.

Who will be elected to the controlling management team? For example, in a corporation, the board of directors controls the company and in a manager managed LLC, the managers control the company, each with one vote.

As a result, a majority partner who, by agreement, only controls only one of three seats on the board of directors doesn't actually have controlling authority over the corporation.

But, a majority partner could elect all three members of the board of directors. Is this something that the partners believe should be addressed in the agreement to protect the minority partners?

Taxes.
The need to address taxes is another critical factor to be considered in preparation of a buy-sell agreement. Pass through entities, such as an "S" corporation or an LLC taxed as a partnership or "S" corporation, cause income to be "imputed" to the partners. Thus, even though the partner gets no cash from the company, she may find that she has to pay the tax on her share of the net profits of the company.

And, with an LLC taxed as a partnership, a transfer of more than 50% of the membership interests causes a "deemed termination" of the partnership for tax purposes. The IRS treats the business as having been terminated, the assets as having been given to the partners at their fair market value (i.e. liquidated) and the partners as having re-contributed those assets to a "new" business. This means each partner pays taxes on the difference between her share of the fair market value of the assets and the amount she contributed to the business just because other partners sold their interests in the business!

To avoid this situation consider requiring certain annual distributions to cover, in part, tax liabilities and limit the ability of majority partners to make a transfer that would result in a "deemed termination."

Also, restrictions must be placed on shareholders so they don't do something that inadvertently terminates a corporation's "S" election.

Compensation.

How will the partners be paid? Salary and profits or profits only? How will the salaries be set? Beware of tax law requirements. Sometimes, partners must be paid a salary (in particular "S" corporations).

It's important to remember that the corporation should pay active partners in two ways: salary and profit distributions. Salaries should be a market rate for the services provided by the partner-employee. Anything less is, effectively, a contribution to the other partners.

Plus, if the business is not profitable because it pays the active partners market salaries, then the business is flawed and should be correct.

It is also important to limit the right of the board of directors to increase or decrease partner employee salaries and other compensation beyond pre-agreed amounts. Majority partners (whether one or a group of partners) can use this technique to funnel money into their pockets that would otherwise go to minority partners as profits.

Finally, owning shares does not give a partner the right to be employed by the corporation. If a minority partner wants to be guaranteed of employment she must have that provision in the partners agreement or in a separate employment agreement.

New Partners.
How (if at all) and at what price are new partners to be brought into the business? Remember, if not prohibited, the board of directors can sell authorized and unissued shares of stock without the shareholders approval.

And even if the articles of incorporation have to be amended to increase the number of authorized shares, the majority partners may be able to do it even if the minority partners object.

Disputes and resolution.
How will disputes be resolved without one of the partners leaving? Often, partners can have legitimate business disagreements without wanting to end their relationship.

Consideration should be given to a deadlock board of directors, trusted advisors who are respected by all partners and who are paid to listen to the competing positions and make a final decision.

Alternatively, the agreement might contain pre-suit mediation or even arbitration; although care must be taken to be sure that a long process is not required when decisions must be made quickly.

Exit strategies.
What is the exit strategy? Where does each partner want to be in 3, 5 or 10 years? Is one talking about going public while the other is looking for a long term life style business?

If there is a majority partner, should the other partners have the right to "tag along" with the majority partner when he sells his stock? Likewise, can the majority partner "drag along" the minority partners if the majority partner wants to sell all of the company's stock?

Growth.
How far and how fast do the partners want the business to grow? Growing a business requires cash – either from financing sources the shareholders may have to guarantee or from operations, requiring the shareholders to forego profit distributions or pay taxes on imputed income without cash. Are the shareholders willing to forego present income and benefits for long term growth?

General expectations.

Why is each partner involved in the business and what does each expect from the other? As was noted in Chapter One, most disputes arise because of unmet expectations. Knowing your partners' expectations means that you can either agree to them or you can mutually decide what expectations are reasonable or appropriate.

An agreement between partners is essential to protect and maximize your business investment. With it you'll be sure each partner is working towards a common goal, that changes in partnership will not harm your business or your personal wealth, and that you and your family will realize the benefit of your business investment.

Chapter Three

Liability and Asset Protection Mistakes

Entrepreneurs form business entities, such as limited liability companies and corporations to protect their personal assets from business debts and obligations. When a business entity is created, structured and used properly, an entrepreneur can limit her risk to money she's invested and left in the business entity.

How does "Limited Liability" work?

With limited liability done right, a business entity is equivalent to a liability shield (as shown on the following figure).

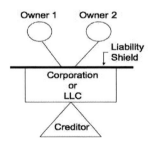

Business owners are protected from business claims and creditors "piercing" through the shield, unless they do something wrong. The creditor can only get access to the assets that are in the entity (the box, above). If nothing (or not enough) is in the entity, the creditor loses because it can't go after the owners.

The Most Common Liability Mistakes.

However, you can make key mistakes with your entity and those business liabilities can become your personal liabilities. Here's how to avoid the most common liability mistakes.

Entity Name.

First, whenever you're doing business it must always be in the <u>exact</u> entity (corporation or LLC) name. If you're in business as *Acme Industrial Enzymes Corporation*, that exact name should appear on all of the company's checks, contracts, invoices and employee business cards.

Never use a shortened name, such as AIE Corp., or any other name unless you've filed a fictitious name registration with the state identifying that the name is owned by Acme Industrial Enzymes Corporation (and not the Acme partners). And, even then, the full name should still appear on all business documents such as contracts, business cards and letterhead.

Executing Contracts.

Next, when signing a contract or other legal document for your business, make sure it is in the entity name; always include your title with your signature (John Smith, President). Also be sure to cross out terms that make the signer a personal guarantor.

Recently, I heard of a situation where a partner was sued when he signed a contract in a slightly different corporate name and didn't include his title. The creditor claimed the partner was acting as a sole proprietor and was personally liable when the corporation didn't pay. The partner paid a settlement when a few simple changes to the name would have protected his money.

Insurance is a Must.

Third, remember that if you, personally, do something that injures another, even on the job, you're probably personally liable.

Take, for example, a one-person bakery. In this example the entrepreneur rises early to bake the bread, then drives around town making deliveries to local shops. One morning he gets into an accident with the delivery truck. Even though the bakery owns the truck and operates the business, the entrepreneur will be liable because he was the one driving.

This means you should always have adequate risk and casualty insurance and a trusted agent to help you find the right policy and the right coverage for your particular business.

Company Asset Management.

Fourth, you can't treat the entity as your personal slush fund. Being in control, you could be liable to its creditors for paying out or taking money improperly.

For example, you can't pay yourself a dividend, remove assets or bleed the entity dry, leaving it penniless so it isn't able to pay its debts. You also can't pay debts the entity owes you and other "insiders" before outside creditors are paid.

You can, however, pay yourself your usual salary and other customary expenses of the business even if creditor claims haven't been paid in full. But, be careful about giving yourself a raise if the business is failing.

Asset transfer problems also arise when there's a holding company and multiple operating companies. The expenses of one operating company can't be paid by another operating company without appropriate accounting documentation. And money and other assets of the operating companies and the holding company must be kept separately.

Corporate Formalities.
Fifth, make sure you follow the formalities for your entity.

Pay the annual fee or franchise taxes so your entity is not administratively dissolved or terminated. Keep your entity records and documents properly. Actually have partner meetings and director meetings and keep minutes. Issue stock certificates and adopt bylaws. Document all changes in management and ownership properly.

Guarantees, Intentional and Accidental.
Finally, avoid guarantees whenever possible.

Many business partners believe they can sign guarantees because they "know" they're not really enforced. Wrong. Guarantees are enforced all the time. If the company fails, the holder of the guarantee will come after the business partner. In some cases the creditor has come after a partner long after she left the business because the guarantee never had an end date.

Also vendors often include guarantee language in (sometimes hidden in) their terms and conditions. You must read all contracts you sign and be sure to eliminate any guarantees you're not willing to provide.

You probably won't get out of guarantees for banks. But don't accept them as "standard" in leases and supplier contracts. The language of the guarantee is critical. Often, you can provide a larger deposit or play one supplier off against another to avoid the guarantee.

Failing to Use An Easy Asset Protection and Tax Reduction Strategy.

Many business partners fail to take advantage of one of the most lucrative and easy ways to protect their assets from creditors and save on taxes.

Many business partners want liability protection and ways to lower taxes, often considering offshore accounts and trusts and other complicated and costly options. Most don't realize that one of the easiest, low cost and most effective ways to accomplish this is a business retirement plan.

Most retirement plans are protected from creditors.

Plus, a business retirement plan will reduce your taxes because the government becomes your savings sponsor. It helps you by letting you use money you'd normally pay in taxes as retirement savings.

For each dollar of income you contribute, the government "lends" you $0.10 to $0.35, depending on your tax bracket.

This is because in order to save $1.00 you have to earn between $1.11 and $1.39. The extra $0.11 to $0.39 are the income taxes you pay.

With certain retirement plans, though, you don't pay those income taxes until you get the money from the plan. The tax is deferred. So, you only have to make $1.00 to invest $1.00.

And, your investment grows tax deferred as well. If you realize a 10% return, all of your earnings stay in your account. None is siphoned off to pay Uncle Sam.

Some of the basic retirement plans available to small businesses include the SEP IRA (Simplified Employee

Pension IRA), the SIMPLE IRA (Savings Incentive Match Plan for Employees) and the individual 401K plan.

For businesses with employees or part-time business partners, the SIMPLE IRA is a good option. With a SIMPLE IRA plan, each eligible employee can contribute between $0 and $10,000 (but not more than the employee's wages), tax deferred. For employees 50 or older, an additional "catch-up" amount can be contributed.

The business either: matches the employee's contribution, up to 3% of her wages, if that is less than or equal to her contribution; or contributes a flat amount of 2% of her wages even if employees make no contribution.

SIMPLE IRA plans permit a two year waiting period for participation at the partner's option. New employees (or those who jump from job to job) would have to wait to participate, as an incentive to stay with the company.

The SIMPLE is also easy and creditor safe. The IRS provides free model paperwork to set up the plan and the money can't be touched by most creditors.

So, why is this a great deal? After all, you still have to contribute for employees.

Say your business has five employees, including you and your spouse. Your salary is $60,000 and your spouse's $20,000. One employee has been with the business for three years, earning $15,000 per year. The other employees are employed less than two years.

To maximize the tax benefit, you and your spouse would each contribute $10,000. The business matches $1,800 for you and $600 for your spouse (3% of wages). Using IRS tax tables (at www.irs.gov), you'd save $5,712 in taxes on the $22,400 invested.

But what about the employees? The two employed less than two years are not eligible. Therefore, no match is made. If the other employee elected to participate and contributed $450 or more, the business would match up to $450.

Even after deducting $450 matched for the employee, the net tax savings to partner and spouse is approximately $5,262. A pretty good deal.

Recent statistics, however, reveal that the vast majority of employees do not make contributions. In that case, no contribution would be made and your net tax savings is greater.

Chapter Four

Trademark Mistakes

The most valuable assets you have are your customers. Lets face it, without them, you don't have a business.

Your customer base is built on goodwill – the value created because customers continue to patronize your business - and trademarks are symbols of that goodwill. As a result, your trademarks (and service marks) are critical business assets that must be protected.

The mistake of failing to protect your trademark is exemplified by Mr. Smith.

Mr. Smith built a successful financial services company from scratch using a particularly good name; one that immediately conveyed the nature of the company's business as well as strength (think something like the Prudential rock logo).

He'd invested tens of thousands of dollars on marketing and advertising using the name and it was really paying off. Business was good.

One early spring afternoon - when Florida weather can't be beat - Mr. Smith was playing golf at a Disney resort wearing a baseball cap with his company's name embroidered on it. This was a part of his marketing.

As he was playing a gentleman approached. The gentleman inquired about Mr. Smith's company. They talked.

This gentleman said he worked for a company by the same name. It was located in New York and he didn't know another company using the same name existed.

The gentleman then asked when Mr. Smith started the business and what he did. It turns out the companies were in the same business. The two exchanged business cards. Mr. Smith thought that was the end of the encounter.

A few weeks later, though, Mr. Smith received a letter from a lawyer representing the New York company. Apparently, that company had registered the name of Mr. Smith's business as a service mark with the U.S. Patent and Trademark Office. The letter demanded Mr. Smith cease using the name immediately.

Stunned, Mr. Smith vowed to fight. After all, he'd spent a lot of money marketing the business under that name.

But the fight didn't last long. Mr. Smith hadn't researched the name before investing the marketing money and hadn't taken any steps to protect it afterward.

As a result, the New York company had the exclusive right to the name.

Mr. Smith had to change the name of his company and, in the process, waste much of the marketing and goodwill he'd built. He had to start over again, building a new company brand.

Key Trademark Knowledge.

To avoid that mistake, there are a few things you need know about trademarks:

<u>The first one to use a trademark usually wins</u>.

If you're using a mark and another business begins using or registers it afterwards, you'll probably have the right to continue your use.

If you've protected it properly, you might even be able to prevent the other business from using it.

To check if your mark or something similar is already being used, check your state registry (www.sunbiz.org, for Florida) and the U.S. Patent and Trademark Office website (www.uspto.gov). Also do a Google search to see if the mark is used elsewhere.

<u>The area where you get the exclusive right to use the trademark depends on how you've protected it.</u>

If you've merely used the mark and haven't filed a registration, you have what is known as "common law" protection. You can use the mark in your trading area plus a reasonable expansion area. You should also identify the mark with a "TM" or an "SM" as appropriate.

On the other hand, if you've registered the mark, you get exclusive use for a defined area. That might be a state or it might be the entire county.

If you register your mark with the U.S. Patent and Trademark Office, you can get exclusive rights to the United States, though, anyone using the mark before your registration can continue their use.

<u>Trademarks apply to different categories of products and services.</u>

Trademarks that appear to be the same or very similar can be used as long as they are in different categories of products or services.

For example, "Lexus" cars and the "Lexis/Nexis" information service can co-exist. Cars and information services are different categories. And the consumers of each won't be confused by the existence of the other.

So, if you find your mark being used in a different industry, you may still be entitled to use it and protect it for your company's goods or services.

Your trademark can't be generic.

Your trademark can't be a generic name for the product or service (e.g., "red apple" for fruit) and can't merely describe something about it (e.g., "baby brie" for small sized brie cheese).

The best mark is arbitrary or fanciful (e.g., "Lexus" for cars, "Xerox" for copy machines), because it doesn't have any relation to the product.

That said, you might be able to protect a mark that merely describes your product/service if you've been using it for some time.

After a mark is used for a time, it may have a "secondary meaning" that relates the descriptive mark to your business. This can happen after extensive marketing or a period of sales.

There's a difference between a service mark and a trademark.

Service marks are used to market a service. Trademarks are attached to a product. Your business name may or may not be a mark.

<u>Register the Words Separate from the Logo</u>.

When registering a mark, if the words and the logo can be registered, it's usually best to register the words of the mark separate from the logo of the mark. This way, if the logo changes over time, the words remain protected.

If the logo and words together were registered and the logo changed, the words alone will have to be re-registered to be protected. And, because there are benefits to having a mark registered for a longer period of time, you don't want to have to re-register your words alone later.

Business owners should protect their service marks and trademarks to protect the long term value of marketing investments (brand) and customer goodwill.

Chapter Five

Employee Mistakes

Employees are absolutely necessary to build a successful growing profitable business. But, one employee mistake can result in major problems and cost your business tens of thousands of dollars.

Aside from morale problems with other employees, a problem employee could sue your business resulting in tens or hundreds of thousands in attorney's fees, not to mention damages you could have to pay to your employee.

Employee Handbook

Part of the key to avoiding employee problems is an employee handbook that describes, in detail, the key provisions of employment.

Take, for example, a company I'll call "Acme."

Acme didn't have an employee handbook. Instead, its owner kept handwritten notes about employee pay rates, reviews, raises, and vacation and sick time. The handwriting wasn't that legible, even to the owner. But, he had it all there and "in his head," so it wasn't a problem for him.

That was until he died suddenly.

When his heirs took over the business it was a mess. The employees claimed they had accumulated hundreds of hours of sick and vacation time. One employee even claimed enough accumulated time to take 8 weeks off from work!

And that didn't include the claims for overtime pay.

Unfortunately, the heirs had no records to refute the claims. So, they were left with two bad choices: give in and pay an outrageous amount of money, or refuse, and have employees leave, disrupting the business, and possibly file wage lawsuits.

The back pay isn't even the bad part about wage lawsuits. Florida law allows employees to recover attorney's fees when they sue your business for failure to pay overtime and minimum amounts they're due. So while the employee may get a few hundred or a couple thousand dollars in back pay, you can be sure the attorneys fees will cost even more.

While the above example may seem extreme, consider your own employee records. Is everything you've spoken about to your employees written in their files? How about their reviews? Are they up to date and accurate? Or, do your files only containing glowing recommendations?

Do you have written time sheets and a policy on overtime? What will happen when a disgruntled employee leaves claiming you failed to pay overtime for the past year or two?

One way to avoid serious problems like these is to have a written employee handbook. With a handbook you won't have "misunderstandings"; all of your team will know what is expected.

Items to Include in Your Employee Handbook:

Your handbook should be comprehensive, addressing all of the terms of employment, including:

- Job description and performance expectations.
- Working hours and overtime, and time sheet requirements.
- Disciplinary procedures.
- Performance review process.
- Complaint handling.
- Benefits.
- Vacation, sick and other time off.
- Salary and compensation payments.
- Expense reimbursement requirements.
- Code of conduct.
- Conflicts of interest policy.
- Sexual harassment policy.

Also, if you've had a particular problem in the past (e.g., travel arrangements, etc.), make sure it's also included and fully addressed.

Every employee should sign a written receipt acknowledging they read the handbook and each change or supplement (when they're distributed).

Practically, the handbook will help avoid legitimate misunderstandings. Strategically, it will help prevent (or at least provide a defense to) unscrupulous lawsuits.

Non-Compete Agreements and Restrictive Covenants

Non-compete and other "restrictive covenant" agreements are your way to prevent employees and contractors from learning your business at your expense, then becoming your competition.

When employees leave, then open shop knowing your prices, customers and way of doing business, they gain an unfair competitive advantage that you paid for!

You can (and should) tailor your restrictive agreement to protect your business. That might mean keeping your employee out of the field entirely or just keeping them from working with your customers.

Without this protection, though, you could lose your entire business.

That business killing mistake was made by ABC Corp. (not its real name). ABC sold and installed industrial products that were manufactured overseas.

A few years ago ABC hired a sales manager, Mr. Jones. Mr. Jones was an experienced sales manager from a different industry. Mr. Jones claimed that he could significantly grow the ABC business. The owner was convinced and wanted Mr. Jones on the team.

As part of the normal hiring process, Mr. Jones was presented with a non-compete/restrictive covenant for his signature. He refused.

But, ABC hired Mr. Jones anyway.

The owner of ABC taught Mr. Jones the ABC business, showing him the ABC prospecting and sales processes, introducing him to the manufacturer's U.S. representative, and giving him the ABC customer list.

Only six months after joining ABC, Mr. Jones quit to pursue "another opportunity."

At first all continued as before with the ABC owner looking for a new sales manager.

Then, a long time customer stopped buying. And others followed, not long after that the manufacturer terminated its relationship with ABC.

Within 3 months, ABC was on its knees and had to layoff most of its employees. What happened?

Once Mr. Jones learned the ABC business (while receiving his ABC salary and benefits), he set up his own company, became a direct representative of the manufacturer and began calling on ABC's customers.

Since he had little overhead, Mr. Jones offered rock bottom pricing. He cut prices to the point where ABC couldn't compete and make a profit.

The simple mistake: permitting the sales manager to be employed without a restrictive covenant.

Key Non-Compete Information.

Non-compete and other restrictive covenants take 4 primary forms:

1.) Non-compete agreements that prohibit competing business activities.

2.) Non-solicitation agreements that prohibit marketing and selling to your customers.

3.) Non-piracy agreements that prohibit soliciting your employees and vendors.

4.) Non-disclosure agreements that prohibit disclosure and use of your company's secret information.

Under Florida law restrictive covenants are enforceable if they meet certain requirements:

- The agreement must be in writing and signed by the employee or contractor.
- The business must be protecting a legitimate business interest such as: valuable secret

information, customer relationships, goodwill, or extraordinary training, to name a few.
- The restriction must be for a reasonable time. For employees, according to the statute a reasonable restriction period is less than 6 months after employment termination and a time more than 2 years after termination of employment is usually not reasonable. In between it depends on the circumstances.
- The restriction must also be reasonable geographically. It can apply only in those areas where you are doing business or have begun to expand. If your client relationships are local, a multi-county restriction in the area is probably reasonable. But not the entire country.
- The restriction must be related to your type of business. Say you sell billing software to dentists, your restriction will generally be practice management software or even healthcare practice management software. But, your restriction can't be all software. Also, be sure to provide a catch-all just in case your business changes.
- Restrictive covenants for present employees must be supported by consideration. In other words, you must give something when they sign the agreement. That could be continued employment or a bonus.

Business owners often make mistakes with continued employment. One employee may resist signing the restrictive covenant. If the employee has been with the company long term or is productive, owners hesitate to fire him if he refuses to sign. But, this leads to trouble because it can make all of the other agreements unenforceable.

In that situation, you have to provide the other employee with consideration for signing the restrictive covenant, typically a bonus check.

You must enforce the agreement if a former employee violates it or you risk losing your rights to enforce any of the agreements.

Restrictive covenants are a legitimate and effective tool to protect your business and the livelihood of your employees. Your agreement must be carefully drafted to meet the legal requirements as well as your particular business needs.

Chapter Six

Employee Becoming Partner Mistakes

Bringing on an employee as a partner into your existing business can be a great tool to retain good talent and grow your business' value. But making it work can be a tricky proposition. If done correctly, your business can grow dramatically. If done wrong, you'll regret it.

Steve had a successful manufacturing business. He'd put in a lot of time and money to build the business, but was looking to step back and slow down. His right hand man, John, seemed to be the right person to run the business. But, John wanted a piece of the action.

To accomplish this Steve gave John a 20% interest of the stock of the business.

Unfortunately, this had a different effect. John decided that, as a partner, he no longer had to put in the long hours he once did. John also thought the business was now his personal slush fund, taking trips, having dinners and doing other things on the business tab. Without Steve and with John living the high life there was no one at the helm and the business stopped growing. That plus the added expenses hit profits hard.

The business faltered and Steve had to come back into the business to right the ship. When he learned what John was doing (or, rather, not doing) he wanted John out. Unfortunately, John wouldn't sell his shares back to Steve at anything near a reasonable price.

Steve had two bad choices: pay John's ransom for the shares (John wanted a lot more than 20% of the business value for the shares) or let John have 20% of the net income and cash from selling the business that Steve had built and had to rebuild. Plus, as the business grew and became more valuable, John would get 20% of Steve's effort. Steve paid the ransom to get rid of John right away.

There are a few things that must be addressed when you admit an employee as a partner.

First, what will the partner pay for the interest in the business? A going concern business has value. To be fair for all parties, that value should be determined by an appraisal of the business. And the new partner should pay that value or participate only in the growth above that value.

Yes, an appraisal is expensive. But, it is much less expensive than selling a part of your business for less than fair market value. Would you sell your home without knowing its market value? Business value is discussed further in Appendix D.

Next, there are tax issues that have to be considered from the outset.

If you merely transfer that value to an employee, the IRS will treat it as compensation. In other words, it will be as if you gave your employee a cash bonus in the amount of the fair market value of the shares and your employee handed that cash to you in exchange for the stock.

That means income taxes, Medicare and, possibly, FICA will have to be paid. If your business is worth very, very little, this won't be a problem. But most going concern businesses have significant value. And the tax problem can be huge.

Let's say that Steve's business was worth $500,000. Steve's transfer of 20% of that business means that the business effectively paid John a $100,000 bonus (ignoring things like minority ownership discounts). John could have to pay $28,000 out of his pocket just to satisfy the income taxes! And the company would have to withhold and pay its share of FICA, if applicable.

Of course, if John paid $100,000 to the company for his shares, there is no tax problem. Had John paid that amount he would truly have had "skin in the game" and, perhaps, treated the business differently.

What if John didn't have the money and Steve wanted to add John as a partner without causing any tax problems?

There are two primary ways to accomplish this: the restricted stock grant or stock option plan.

Restricted Stock Grant.

Using a restricted stock grant, John would be issued all of his shares from the company at the time of the grant. But those shares would be lost (the company literally cancels the shares) if John didn't meet certain conditions, with less shares cancelled as time progressed.

Usually the condition is continued employment. So, if John was terminated two years into a four year employment condition, half the shares would be cancelled.

Now, John would still have to pay income tax. However, his "income" would be less than the fair market value of the shares because he could lose them. And John would have a couple of options on how to treat that income. Plus the company could pay John a bonus for the taxes

Stock Option.

With a stock option, on the other hand, John would be granted the right to buy one share of the company's stock from the company for each option granted, at today's fair market value (or just a bit higher, depending on John's position with the company). Assuming all elements of the plan are prepared correctly, the tax code allows the grant of the options to John without the grant being income to John for tax purposes.

Stock options typically vest (i.e., they're able to be exercised) over 4 or 5 years of employment, with no options vesting until one full year has been completed.

If John doesn't perform adequately in the first year, he wouldn't have had the ability to purchase any stock.

And John can hold the options for up to 5 or 10 years. He can exercise the options just before the company sells in a "cashless" exercise to get the benefit from the company's sale without having to invest any cash.

Both restricted stock and stock options should be accompanied by an appropriate written employment agreement.

Finally, how do you keep the business if John leaves or you want him to leave? What happens if John is fired after a year or two or three and he's exercised options or the forfeiture provisions of a restricted stock grant have gone away?

This is when the shareholders agreement is required. With a shareholders agreement, the company and the other shareholders can restrict John's ability to sell the shares and require that he resell them to the company.

Furthermore, a shareholders agreement can be structured to prevent John from causing problems by voting his shares or exercising certain rights he has as a shareholder.

For example, if Steve wants to sell the company through a stock sale to get the tax benefits, John could refuse to sell his shares. Without a shareholders agreement, there is nothing Steve could do.

Other similar situations exist. Chapter Two discusses shareholders agreements in detail.

By considering all of the issues involved in admitting an employee as a co-owner and preparing appropriate written documentation, the company can grow and become more profitable without the downside risk.

Chapter Seven

Franchise Buyer Mistakes

Many people consider franchising as an option to go into business ownership or expand an already existing business.

If you're thinking about buying into a franchise, I urge you to proceed carefully. This path is risky if not done right.

Between the franchise fee - which can range from $25,000 to $100,000 (and sometimes even more) - the start-up costs, working capital, and the 6 months to 1 year of living expenses (before the business supports you), franchisees can end up spending $50,000 to over $300,000.00 to get into and start a franchised business.

That's often much more than it would cost to start an independent (non-franchised) business or to buy an existing business.

Franchise buyers justify the additional expense because they believe franchise systems give them a higher chance of success.

Most of them have never owned a business before. They rightfully believe that small businesses are very risky. So they want the security of a support system. They want to be in charge of their own destiny, yet have someone to rely upon for help.

SBA Research Shows Franchises Fail at a Higher Rate than Independent Businesses!

But are franchises truly less risky? Do they provide security? Are they worth the money?

Believe it or not, according to research conducted by the U.S. Small Business Administration the answer may be NO!

SBA research has shown that independent small businesses have a better chance of surviving than small franchised businesses!

What?

That's right. The SBA research discovered that franchised businesses had a 6% higher failure rate than the rate for independent businesses.

According to the SBA research:
- Starting an independent business was less risky than buying into a franchise system.

- Independent entrepreneurs are in business longer and do better financially than franchised businesses.

Other SBA research also determined that 56% of franchise systems did not exist within 4 years after they started franchising, and a full 75% of franchise systems did not exist within 10 years.

That means that more than half of franchisors get out of franchising within 4 years and 3 out of 4 are out of franchising within 10 years!

Two recent articles in Entrepreneur Magazine (January 2010 issue) cataloged several recent franchise concepts that have failed (including eBay drop-off stores, meal preparation stores and dating franchises) and how a franchisee dealt with the franchisor's bankruptcy (Cork and Olive franchise system).

What happens to the franchisees that bought into those franchise systems?

Even though they paid tens of thousands of dollars of franchise fees for support and assistance, they no longer have it. If they buy products from the franchisor, they can't get inventory. And they're left on their own.

Are all franchisors are at risk? The answer is that not all franchise systems are the same. There are good ones and bad ones.

How can you tell the difference?

You have to be sure that: (1) you're getting what you need to get into business faster and make more money than you would in an independent business; (2) once you grow that business, you'll be able exit it and realize the wealth you've created; and (3) the franchisor has staying power.

How do you know which franchisor will help you create a great business and which one will leave you in a financial bomb crater?

You have to know what the franchisor is providing for the franchise fee, and understand the information in the Uniform Franchise Offering Circular (UFOC) and the Franchise Agreement.

The 3 Things Every Franchise MUST Provide.
Every franchise must provide each franchisee at least these three elements:
- Recognizable Registered Trademark.
- True Turnkey Systems.
- Valuable (and inexpensive) Business Assistance.

These three elements enable a good franchisor to open new franchise locations, to hire and train employees effectively and to get new customers quickly. Remember, buying into a franchise means starting a new business from scratch. These three elements are supposed to get you up and running and make you successful faster than doing it without the franchise.

Trademark.

The trademark brings customers to the franchised business because its readily recognized by the market the franchise serves. If that market doesn't know the trademark or, god forbid, the mark doesn't come with a good reputation, don't buy the franchise. You'll be better off with an independent business.

(By the way, getting in on the "ground floor" when the franchisor doesn't have a well known mark, isn't a good deal. You'll spend your money to develop their mark and you won't get the long term benefit from doing it.)

The trademark should also be registered with the United States Patent and Trademark Office. Registration means that a government lawyer has reviewed and approved the mark, that the mark has been published for opposition and, that the mark, once registered for a period of time, will get special protection. In other words, there's a much higher likelihood that the mark is valid and can be protected by the franchisor.

Turnkey Systems.

Turnkey systems enable franchisees to work in a business where they have little or no experience and to get things up and running quickly. You can determine whether the franchise systems are adequate by talking with (and secret shopping) other franchisees.

In my opinion, prospective franchisees must do these visits before committing to a franchisor. You have to physically shop, visit and talk with multiple franchisees in all franchise territories, near and far, before you buy.

If the franchisee's employees aren't following the system or the franchisee says something about taking more time than expected to get up and running, this is a red flag the franchisor's systems may not be as good as they should be. If there's any indication that the sales and marketing system isn't as good as it should be, you shouldn't buy the franchise.

Assistance.
When you're having a problem with your business, you want someone who understands your business on the other end of the phone or visiting your location and who can provide meaningful suggestions and assistance. You don't want to call the franchisor only to be read what's in the operations manual.

You can determine whether the franchisor provides appropriate assistance in franchisee interviews and by investigating the background and experience of the people the franchisor uses to provide that assistance.

You Must Read and Understand the UFOC.
You MUST read and understand all of the Information provided in the Uniform Franchise Offering Circular (affectionately known as the UFOC). Although it may seem

like pages and pages of legalese and seemingly irrelevant and useless information, you have to carefully read the UFOC and know what to look for. The UFOC will tell you a lot about the prospective franchisor and the franchise system.

You have to know what's there that shouldn't be and what needs to be there but isn't. You have to know the little tricks that franchisors use to make more money and harm your profitability. You have to know what things that seem harmless come back to bite you weeks and sometimes years later. You have to know the signs that a franchisor is likely to fail. You have to know how much the franchise truly costs.

What's Your Franchisor Partner's Real Cut of the Action?

For instance, how much of a "partner" is the franchisor in your business? I say partner because the franchisee gets its money off the top. It's an additional expense that is paid first and that reduces your net profit.

If you say 5% or 6% because that's the royalty rate, you're wrong.

Instead, you've got to add the royalty rate and the advertising fees (because you don't get to say how the advertising money is spent and, very often, it won't be used to grow your business, only to build "brand awareness" for the franchisor) and compare them against the bottom line you expect from the franchised business.

For example, if the franchise you're considering charges a royalty rate of 6% and the advertising rate of 2%, and you anticipate the bottom line net profit for a business of this type, after paying yourself a reasonable salary, should be 15% of gross revenue (for an independent business), then the franchisor will be getting 8% of gross revenue and your net profit should be about 7% of gross revenue. This means that the franchisor gets 53% of the profit and you get 47% of the profit.

Of course, you have to include other fees and charges in that calculation. Many franchisors require franchisees to buy supplies from franchisor vendors. If those supplies are overpriced (typically because the franchisor gets a 'commission' from the vendor), then the extra charges have to be added into the franchisor payments.

You also have to know what you're getting for all that money and what it would cost you to buy those benefits outside a franchise.

If the franchised business in the above example generates gross revenue of $750,000 annually, then you'll be paying the franchisor about $60,000 per year and you'll net about $52,500 (excluding your salary).

You have to ask: "What products or services could you buy for an independent business for $60,000 per year?" and "Is the franchisor obligated by the franchise agreement (no verbal "promises accepted") to give you at least those products and services?"

This example ignores the up-front franchise fee and other franchise specific expenses, which should be added to those numbers.

The above examples are only a couple of the business and legal issues to be considered. Other areas include renewal provisions, non-compete provisions, whether you have the right to require the franchisor to enforce the territory restrictions, franchisor assistance obligations and whether the franchisor can impose changes on you that require more capital investment.

What if the Franchisor Won't Change the Deal?

Frankly, reviewing the UFOC and the Franchise Agreement are areas where you've got to get experienced professional advice. Even though franchisors are often reluctant - or flat out refuse - to change any provisions of the franchise agreement, you have to know what you're getting into before you commit your hard earned dollars so you can evaluate the alternatives from starting an independent business to buying a going concern business.

Using these methods will help you determine if a franchise is worth your investment and help you avoid losing tens or hundreds of thousands of dollars on an inadequate or failing franchise, or a franchise that's just a plain bad deal.

Chapter Eight

Business Growth Mistakes – Organic Growth

How You Should be Creating Exponential Growth for Your Business

Most business owners make the mistake of focusing on only one way to organically grow their businesses: get more customers. Usually this means expensive advertising campaigns that yield questionable results.

Unfortunately, these business owners don't do anything with the two other ways to grow a business, (getting customers to buy more, and buy more often) even though those ways are less expensive than getting new customers. And, by focusing on all of the three ways to grow a business, you achieve exponential results.

Say you have 100 customers who each purchase $1,000 on average from you each year. Your gross revenue last year was $100,000.

If you only focus on growing the number of customers by 10% - say by additional advertising or other marketing campaign - you'll gross $110,000 next year. A 10% increase. Not bad, but you can do better.

How? Well, what if you also grew the average amount each customer purchased?

Growing the average purchase by 10% to $1,100 means your 110 customers purchase an average of $1,100, for a total gross revenue of $121,000 – a 21% total increase.

Getting better. But, you can do more.

What if you could also increase the average number of times each purchased by 10%? Now your 110 customers are buying an average of $1,100 of products or services 1.1 times per year from you.

You've increased your sales to $133,100 - a 33.1% total increase.

Plus, increasing the average purchase and the number of purchases from existing customers is much easier than getting new customers to buy.

Increasing the amount purchased and the number of purchases are based on the types of customers you have, what you offer to them and how you maintain your relationship with them.

The Right Customers
First you must have the "right" customers.

You'll probably notice that most of your profit (something like 80%) comes from very few of your customers (probably around 20% to 30%). Interestingly, these customers are usually the ones who value what you sell and willingly pay your prices for it. I call these "A" customers.

Keeping "A" customers, getting rid of the bad customers and getting more "A" customers will both increase the average purchase of each customer and reduce the need to get more new customers. It also makes your business more enjoyable and easier to work. Your "A" customers are much more likely to buy more and buy longer.

Getting rid of the non-"A" customers can be tough. Many business owners are reluctant to send customers with money packing. But, doing so will free up time for your new "A" customers and result in business and profit growth.

I know, it's counter-intuitive, but it is true.

One way to do this, if you already have too much business, is to increase your prices. You'll have fall out of the not-so-good customers. However, the increased revenue from those who remain will make up for the customers you lost.

Also, because you now know what "A" customers are like, it'll be easier to find and keep them and the new higher rates. That will create an overall gain.

Increasing the Dollar Amount of Each Purchase

Increasing the amount of each purchase can be accomplished a number of ways.

Consider packaging a product or service with additional services that might not normally be purchased at once.

Arrange for a good, better, best product or service structure. Offer larger units of products or services.

Or, arrange with a third party to provide complementary products or services to your customers with you receiving part of the purchase price (sort of like a commission).

Increasing Number of Purchases

Increasing the number of purchases is about keeping in touch with (i.e., marketing to) your "A" customers on a regular and consistent basis.

You might think that most customers no longer frequent a business because they were treated poorly or dissatisfied. That is not the case. Most leave because they were neglected.

This is very costly for your business. Once you've developed your relationship with a customer, it is much easier and less expensive to get that customer to do business with you again than it is to find a new customer.

Make sure your "A" customers hear from you at least quarterly. You don't have to be fancy; a simple letter or e-news-letter will do. Give them useful information or a valuable outcome, preferential treatment, free gifts or special deals. Make it worthwhile for them to keep doing business with you and make sure they remember you.

The other benefit of keeping in communication with your "A" customers is referrals. Your "A" customer hang around with other people who are like them and who could become new "A" customers for you. Because they're happy with your product or service, they're your best salespeople. Just asking for referrals from them can yield better results with far less expense than an advertising campaign.

Focusing on all three ways to grow a business will yield exponential results. And continuing and strengthening your relationship with existing customers will pay off for you and them.

Chapter Nine

Business Growth Mistakes – Growth by Business Acquisition

Even when you use all of the methods described in Chapter Eight, growing a business organically can be a time consuming process.

One way to grow a business quickly is to buy an existing complementary or competitors business. Often, because there may be areas of duplication in both businesses (such as back room operations), you can make more profit from an acquired business than the seller will have made with it.

Unfortunately, many entrepreneurs make the mistake of never considering this as an alternative.

In this Chapter, we'll discuss this viable and potentially very lucrative growth option and where the most common mistakes are made.

Of course, the process is not without risk. Many businesses that are for sale are over-priced and have big problems. Some are on the brink of closing their doors and some business owners are downright dishonest.

So, as with any big purchase you've got to do your homework. You don't want to buy the seller's problems or, worse, pay for something that's dying and might infect your business.

The Process: An Overview.

First, though, it's critical that you know that buying a business is not like buying a home or commercial property.

The biggest difference is that real estate has value even if it isn't producing income. Small businesses without cash flow, on the other hand, are usually worth little or nothing.

Buying a business today is about buying customer relationships (also called goodwill) and cash flow from those customers generated by the operation and management of the business. This is often referred to as a "going concern."

Unfortunately, the desks, equipment, files and inventory may have a very low value apart from the business. So, most of your money will be buying what you can't touch – the future expectation that money will come into the business.

Another difference between buying a business and buying a home is how the sale is completed.

If you've purchased a home, you know that the purchase and sale contract is generally a standard document with fill-in-the-blank spots. Here in Florida, the Bar Association and the Division of Real Estate have come up with a standard agreement that real estate agents can help buyers complete. It's called the "FAR/BAR".

This is also the case with a home mortgage. You don't negotiate the terms of the promissory note or mortgage. Rather, the person closing the sale just presents the preprinted "Fannie Mae" approved documents for your signature.

Well, that is certainly not the case when buying a business. The differences between businesses are so great, there are no true "standard" contracts.

Rather, you have to be sure that all of the promises made by the seller about that particular business are in the contract. This situation was exemplified in Chapter One with the cement plant buyer.

The common and costly mistakes made when buying a business to grow include:
- Failing to understand and complete all of the steps of the buying process.
- Not giving yourself enough time to fully analyze the business.
- Relying on the advice of people who don't have experience or who are financially involved in the deal.
- "Falling in love" with the business.
- Becoming friends with the seller.
- Failing to get help from a lawyer and an accountant.

The Steps to Buying a Business.

Broadly speaking, the steps to buying a business are:

- Find a suitable business.
- Conduct a preliminary investigation.
- Make an offer.
- Conduct a detailed investigation.
- Prepare, negotiate and sign contracts.
- Get third party approvals and consents and wrap up loose ends.
- Close the deal.

Not all of these steps are separate. Nor will you always proceed from the first step directly through to the last. Often, one step won't be fully completed before you being the next. Sometimes, you'll do the steps out of order or combine two steps into one.

The target business will dictate what steps are appropriate and in what order you'll need to accomplish them.

Finding a Suitable Business.

The first step of buying a business to expand your current business is to find your "target": the business to buy.

The three variables to guide you to the right targets are:

- What type of business makes sense?
- How much money do you have for the purchase?
- How will you make contact?

What type of business makes sense?

To make sure you don't make the mistake of acquiring a company that doesn't offer the most benefit for your business, this strategic question must be addressed first. The answer to this depends on what aspect of your business you're looking to improve and grow.

If you're looking to expand your customer base (the most common reason), then a competitor in the same market area, a business outside your market area or a business selling complementary products or services to yours all make sense.

A business selling complementary products gives you two growth options: sell your current products to that business' customer base <u>and</u> sell that business' products to your customers.

But, don't make the mistake of buying a company with a product or service that is too different from the ones you're company are currently selling. Otherwise, you'll have to increase your expenses and team expertise to serve the target's customers, reducing the overall benefit.

When buying a competitor you can both expand your customer list and decrease advertising and back room expenses for an overall increase in bottom line profitability for each sale and increase your customer base.

How much money do you have for the purchase?

When it comes to the amount of money you have to invest in the purchase, you don't do yourself or anyone else any favors by "puffing." This is a huge mistake that will cause you to waste your time and money looking at deals you can't make happen. And, if you do get into a deal that's above your head, you could kill the target and your company in the process. You'll be strapped for cash and vulnerable to even the slightest financial hiccup.

Despite what some infomercials would have you believe, there aren't many "no-money-down" business deals. Plus, those that I've seen are usually dying and the owner is looking to get out at all costs and to dump the liabilities.

Of course, that doesn't mean you need or should pay all cash for your purchase. Most sellers over price their businesses and say they want an "all cash" deal. But, very few transactions happen that way.

You'll need to figure working capital into your calculations. With an asset sale (described below) the seller retains all of the bank accounts and cash, and sometimes the accounts receivable. So, you'll need to cover the business expenses for the first 30 or 60 days, depending on how quickly the business collects its sales and how much inventory it holds.

The bottom line is this: Without enough cash you're setting yourself up for failure.

How will you make contact?

The answer to this question sounds pretty straight forward.

But isn't as easy as it first seems. Business owners don't usually stick a sign in the window as you might if you were selling a house.

Keeping secret the fact that a business is for sale is important to the owner. If word got out, employees might wonder about the future, perhaps even find new jobs, and customers might look for alternative suppliers. Also, competitors could use this information to lure customers or spread rumors to suppliers and vendors. All-in-all, not good for business.

So, the business owner faces a dilemma: how does she market the business without letting people know the business is for sale.

Of course, you can (and should) contact specific businesses that you identify as potential targets. However, for the reasons describe above, many business owners won't talk to you for fear the word would get out.

Recently a client was looking to acquire a direct competitor and asked me to make contact. Part of his requirement was that he not be identified until the competitor indicated an interest in selling. The competitor wouldn't talk until I identified the potential buyer. I couldn't per my client's instructions, so we had to try an alternative approach.

For those and other reasons (such as help with determining how much the business is worth), most business sellers use business brokers to market their businesses.

So, knowing how to avoid mistakes with business brokers is essential.

<u>Working with a Business Brokers.</u>

The most common mistakes entrepreneurs make when working with a business broker are:
- Not understanding the type of brokerage relationship.
- Believing the broker is their "advisor."
- Failing to remember that brokers only get paid when a deal closes.
- Failing to remember that broker compensation increases (and decreases) with the selling price.

You must keep these mistakes in mind whenever you're getting the broker's advice.

Now, before you go off thinking I don't like business brokers, wait a minute. I'm not saying that all brokers pursue the buck over your well being. To the contrary, there are many excellent experienced brokers who do the right thing, even when it costs them a deal. You just have to know who you're dealing with and what they're obligated to do for you and for the other party.

To get unbiased advice, the person giving that advice to you (whether broker, attorney or consultant) must have what is known as "a duty of loyalty" or fiduciary duty to you and no one else. When this exists your advisor is legally obligated to put your interests above his and everyone else.

For example, duty of loyalty is always present with an attorney-client relationship. It is sometimes present with a business broker depending on the specific type of legal relationship you have with the broker.

Business Broker Legal Relationships.

In Florida and many other states, business brokers are required to be licensed. The license law defines several relationships between brokers and the people they work with. The two most common are single agent and transaction broker.

The type of relationship between you and the broker must be dealt with upfront so you know what you can expect.

Don't make assumptions. Get the type of relationship disclosed in writing. In Florida there are specific notice forms the broker can use.

Single Agent.

The first type of relationship a broker can have with his customer is known as "single agent." This means the broker has a duty of loyalty (also known as a fiduciary duty) to his customer. Usually, it's the seller. But, his customer can be either the seller or the buyer, no matter who's paying. In some states, this is the only type of broker relationship.

When dealing with a single agent broker of the seller, everything you, as the buyer, say to the broker must be relayed by the broker to the seller. In other words, when you're talking with a single agent broker of the seller, you're talking directly to the seller.

For example, if you were to tell the seller's single agent broker that you'd be willing to pay more to buy the business, the broker must, by law, tell the seller. So be careful what you say.

A single agent broker for the seller also can't advise you of a fair price for the business or how the asking price was determined.

Also, be aware: just because you call a broker who isn't the listing agent, that broker may still be the single agent broker for the seller. In that case the broker would be a sub-agent of the single agent broker for the seller.

Transaction Broker.

In Florida most business brokers operate as transaction brokers. A transaction broker does not owe anyone - buyer or seller - a fiduciary duty. They're in it to make the deal work.

However, as transaction broker the broker must keep certain information confidential. If you were to tell a transaction broker you'd be willing to pay more, she'd be obligated to keep that secret.

By knowing what the parties are truly willing to do, honest transaction brokers can move seller and buyer closer together by dealing with problems of each side. For this reason, transaction brokers can be better suited to facilitate buyer and seller reaching a mutually beneficial deal.

But it is important not to mistake a transaction broker for an advisor. A transaction broker isn't your advisor because he doesn't owe you that duty of loyalty. So you have to be careful of the advice or suggestions you get from a transaction broker and you definitely need a knowledgeable experienced advisor other than the transaction broker.

Dealing with the Business Broker.

Expect to meet with a business broker, in person, at his office to discuss your qualifications, experience, earning expectations, financial resources and the types of businesses in which you're interested. Once your broker learns a bit about you, talks about the process and does a preliminary reality check, he'll have a few documents for you to complete and sign.

Many of these documents are designed to separate serious buyers from tire kickers. Buying a business takes work. If a prospective buyer won't do preliminary paperwork, it is unlikely she'll ever buy a business. And, because the broker is only paid once a sale is made, they're not interested in spending time with people who aren't committed to buying.

The broker will also have you sign a confidentiality agreement for each business you want to look at. This is your agreement not to disclose the information provided to you about that business. Sometimes, that includes a non-circumvention agreement (where you agree not to try to buy the business from the seller after being introduced by the broker) and a disclosure notice describing the type of relationship between you and the broker (single agent, transaction broker, etc.).

Conducting a Preliminary Investigation.

When the paperwork is complete and you've been qualified, the broker will show you listings. Or you'll start the process of generating inquiries for businesses that aren't currently listed yourself.

For listed business, the "showing" begins with an information package or listing description prepared by the listing broker and seller describing the type of business and providing some key financial information.

For businesses that you target and aren't listed with a broker, you'll want to get this information informally through a conversation with the owner.

The preliminary information you'll need includes the business' financial results for the past three years, the types and amounts of assets being sold, a copy of the lease, information about how the business differentiates itself and the reason the seller has decided to sell (although what you're told may not be the real reason).

For the financial information with a broker listed business, you should expect to get numbers for gross sales, general expense categories (but not individual expenses), adjusted net or owner's benefit, the value of assets and leasehold improvements and the amount of inventory at hand. You'll be able to determine the net profit percentage by comparing the adjust net to gross sales, the growth of sales over the past three years and the amount of inventory on hand. You'll also typically be provided with information about the leased space size and amount of rent. You should assume the information is accurate (the time to check the accuracy is later) and analyze it to determine whether the business is healthy, viable and right for you.

When working with a broker you'll probably look at one or several of these information packages or listing descriptions and select a few businesses for in-person visits.

The broker will arrange and typically accompany you on these visits.

Sellers range from those who readily and easily provide you with all the information you request and tell you everything about the business, to those who won't say much until an offer is on the table.

Buyers are often surprised to learn that they usually don't get to make a detailed inspection of the numbers before making an offer. The process is designed to see whether there can be a "meeting of the minds" between buyer and seller, usually on price and payment terms, before a lot of time and effort are spent on investigating the details of the business (known as due diligence) and before the seller has to disclose too much confidential or personal information.

Sellers don't want their tax returns, financial statements, and other confidential business and personal information handed out to a lot of people.

Does this mean there's no negotiation? Absolutely not. Offers need not be, and usually are not, at the asking price or on the asking terms. But no information need be exchanged unless the offer is something the seller is willing to accept.

Making an Offer.
If everything seems to be in order and you like a business, you'll next move to making an offer. Offers are made through a signed contract or a letter of intent.

Your contract must contain provisions that reflect the terms of your deal. It must hold the seller to his promises about the business and it must allow you to get out of the contract (before you close) if you aren't happy (after you perform an in-depth investigation). Business purchase contract issues are discussed below in the section titled: The Purchase and Sale Contract.

Some fill-in-the-blank contracts will only let you out of the deal if the business' numbers are not within 95% of the financial information provided. This isn't good enough. What if you discover a problem with some other aspect of the business, such as the lease or supplier contracts? With that contract you'd be stuck. Due diligence is discussed below in the section titled: Detailed Investigation.

Next, no matter what, you must read and fully understand the contract or letter of intent before you sign it.

Purchase and sale contracts are enforceable, and have been enforced, against both buyers and sellers who've reneged on their obligations. Don't assume you can get out of it or have a 3 day right of recession.

Making an offer through a letter of intent instead of a contract is typically the easiest path for the buyer. A letter of intent is usually non-binding except for secrecy obligations. It sets out the major terms, including price, seller financing and significant promises about the state of the business (also called representations and warranties) that the seller is making about the business, such as, gross income and net profit.

But, a letter of intent is not perfect. First, the Seller may not think you're serious. Next, because it is non-binding, if another, better, offer comes along, the seller could jump to the better deal. Many sellers will use your LOI to shop other interested prospective buyers for a better deal.

Finally, it will take more time and may cost more to use a letter of intent.

So using the right contract is usually the right way to make an offer.

How much should you pay?

Of course, the biggest issues in making an offer are price and terms. Many, if not most, small businesses are over priced. The seller has an inflated idea about the value of his business.

Sellers also demand all cash or a large down payment. This can be because the broker is unwilling to have a realistic conversation with his seller or because the seller needs the cash or doesn't want to finance more than is absolutely necessary.

So, you'll have to negotiate both price and terms. Business valuation is discussed in detail in Appendix D.

Structuring the Deal: Asset Purchase or Stock Purchase?

There are two primary ways that businesses are purchased: a stock purchase or an asset purchase. The most common, by far, is an asset purchase.

Consider a manufacturing business with two owners, Smith and Jones. The business is operated through a corporation, Seller Corporation, where Smith and Jones are the only shareholders (figure 1). Seller Corporation owns the business and all of the contracts, bank accounts and assets are in the name of Seller Corporation.

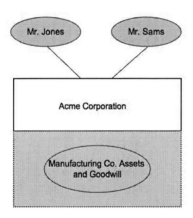

Figure 1

Smith and Jones decide to sell the manufacturing business and Mr. Bucks decides he'd like to try his hand as a manufacturer.

Stock Purchase.

The first available option is a stock purchase. In this arrangement, Smith and Jones, as shareholders (the owners of S&J Corporation), enter a stock purchase agreement with Mr. Bucks (figure 2). Mr. Bucks buys the stock directly from Smith and Jones, by paying the purchase price to Smith and Jones. Smith and Jones then transfer their shares of stock to Mr. Bucks.

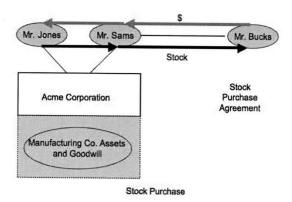

Figure 2

Once the sale is completed, Mr. Bucks is the sole shareholder of S&J Corporation and, through it, the manufacturing business (Figure 3).

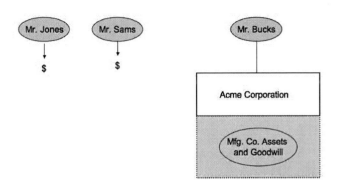

Stock Purchase
Figure 3

The tax situation with a stock sale is straight forward. Smith and Jones pay tax on the "gain" they receive (basically, the profit) from Mr. Bucks at capital gains tax rates, which, as I write this, is 15%.

Stock purchase transactions work well where there are many (more than five) owners and one wants out or there are non-transferable contracts.

For example, a few years ago, two men who owned a technology consulting business used a stock purchase to amicably part ways.

These owners had built a successful company with multiple consultants calling on customers throughout the Orlando metropolitan area. One was the outside sales person and the other the inside administrative partner.

They began to have disagreements over the amount of work each was doing and the management of the company. One wanted the other to be in the office and the other wanted to be selling to new accounts.

But, even though the owners weren't getting along, the company itself had a good reputation, healthy client base and distinctive name.

So, rather than start from scratch, one owner agreed to buy the stock of the other. This allowed the purchaser to continue the business, benefit from the goodwill with the customers and avoid any competition from the seller. The seller was able to get money for his new non-competing business.

Asset Purchase.

The second and most common method is the asset purchase. With this arrangement, the corporation owned by Smith and Jones sells all of its assets to a corporation owned by Mr. Bucks (we'll call this "Bucks company") (Figure 4).

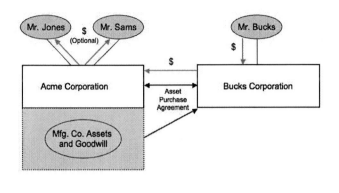

Asset Purchase
Figure 4

All or, in most cases, a portion of the purchase price (the down payment plus working capital) is put into the Bucks Corporation's bank account by Mr. Bucks. Then, Bucks Corporation writes a check to the S&J Corporation (owned by Smith and Jones). S&J Corporation then transfers all of its assets to the Bucks Corporation. And, finally, S&J Corporation distributes the money it receives to Smith and Jones.

Usually, these assets include all of the furniture, fixtures and equipment (also known as "FF&E") of S&J Corporation, its business name and other IP and goodwill. Bucks Corporation also assumes all or a portion of S&J Corporation's contracts and liabilities, including, the lease for S&J Corporation's facility or offices.

When the asset purchase is complete, the business and assets are owned by Bucks Corporation and S&J Corporation owns the cash from the purchase price or, most often, the cash and a promissory note from Bucks Corporation (Figure 5). The note represents the seller financing of the purchase by S&J Corporation and its shareholders.

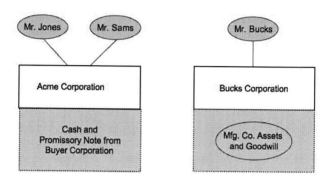

Asset Purchase
Figure 5

The tax situation for Smith and Jones with an asset purchase transaction is a bit more complicated. It depends on whether S&J Corporation is taxed as a "C" corporation or an "S" corporation (for more information on "C" and "S" corporations see Appendix C), the profits of S&J Corporation to date, and the value of the FF&E and amount of depreciation taken.

If S&J Corporation is a "C" corporation, then S&J Corporation pays taxes on the gain from the sale of the assets, usually around 35%. Then when S&J Corporation pays a dividend to Smith and Jones, they include their dividend as income on their tax return, and pay approximately 15% tax.

As a result, the income is taxed twice, once to the corporation and then again to the shareholder when they receive the proceeds. The tax rates vary, but the combined rate is approximately 44.75%, much greater than the 15% capital gains rate paid in the stock purchase transaction.

If S&J Corporation is an "S" corporation, then Smith and Jones pay taxes on the S&J Corporation's gain and profits. Unlike the "C" corporation, this income is taxed only once to Smith and Jones. The tax rates vary based on the factors listed above. But, a portion of the income will probably be taxed at ordinary income rates (Approximately 28 to 35%) and, again, the overall tax rate will be more than the capital gains rate of 15% used for the stock purchase.

In short, the tax advantages of a stock sale benefit the seller.

Why an Asset Sale?
So, why are small business sales almost always structures as asset sales?

The two most important reasons that buyers purchase only the assets of the business are:
- Liabilities.
- Depreciation.

Liabilities.

If you buy the stock of the S&J Corporation, you are stuck with and have to pay all of its liabilities, known and unknown. Whatever money you pay for that stock is at risk for those liabilities. If you don't pay them, you could lose your entire investment in the business.

On the other hand, if you buy just the assets of the business at arms-length (i.e. no insider or sweetheart deals), you can take over the business, but avoid most of the liabilities. The liabilities have to be paid by the seller before it distributes the money from the purchase price to its shareholders. Otherwise, the creditors can go after the shareholders for the money they received from the seller.

So, if you pay a reasonable price for the business, you don't have to worry about a lawsuit coming up a week after you take over the business. If it does, it's the seller's problem.

However, if the seller doesn't pay a vendor or sold a defective product, you won't be legally liable. (I say legally liable because you may want to or, as a practical matter, have to pay these kinds of claims to maintain the good name of the business, nonetheless.)

Some liabilities cannot be left behind even in an asset purchase. For example, you can be liable for certain environmental claims. And, any claims that are liens on the assets you just bought must be satisfied or you could lose those assets (See information on Liens and Encumbrances).

Depreciation.

Depreciation is the right of a business to deduct from its income each year a portion of the cost of its tangible assets. It is permitted to allow the business to recover a portion of the cost to replace the asset as the asset wears out.

So, in simple terms, if a restaurant purchases a pizza oven with a seven year useful life for $49,000.00, the business can deduct $7,000 (one-seventh of the cost of the machine) from its income each year for seven years. This way the business will, in theory, have $49,000 to purchase a new oven when the current one wears out.

Now, the oven will probably continue to work after it has been fully depreciated, but that doesn't matter. It only means the business cannot take the depreciation deduction.

As you can see, if there is a large amount of furniture, fixtures and equipment used in the business, the deduction can be substantial.

Depreciation is basically tax-free income for the business. And, in some cases, the tax law allows a business to accelerate the depreciation deduction or take it all in one year.

This type of accelerated depreciation using deduction in the year you buy your business could enable you to recover all of your employment income taxes for that year.

Remember, in a stock purchase the owner of the asset – S&J Corporation– doesn't change. The only thing that changes is the owner of S&J Corporation. So, S&J Corporation just continues deducting as it did before you bought the stock.

So, if during the time Smith and Jones owned the stock of S&J Corporation, S&J Corporation depreciated the assets to zero, S&J Corporation (and indirectly you) won't be able to take any depreciation. Even if the S&J Corporation hasn't fully depreciated all assets to zero, it certainly has taken some depreciation during the time it was owned by Smith and Jones. That tax-free income is now unavailable to you.

With a stock purchase, you won't get the full benefit of depreciating the assets.

On the other hand, in an asset sale, Buyer Company gets to depreciate the entire purchase price as permitted by the tax law.

Plus, Buyer company gets an added bonus. In addition to depreciating FF&E, it also gets to depreciate the goodwill of the purchased business.

Now, "goodwill" is a term accountants use. It is the difference between the price Buyer Company paid for the business and the fair market value of the tangible assets including FF&E. In theory, goodwill reflects the value of the going concern aspect of the business and the relationship between the business and its customers.

Goodwill is depreciated over 15 years, a relatively long time. Nonetheless, being able to depreciate it still provides additional tax benefit for Buyer company and, indirectly Mr. Buyer.

Say Mr. Buyer purchases the restaurant through an asset sale for $350,000. Of that amount $140,000 is allocated to the furniture, fixtures and equipment (FF&E) and the balance to goodwill.

If we assume that all of the FF&E has a useful life of seven years, then for the next seven years the first $34,000.00 of income is tax free. The first $20,000 represents the amortization of $140,000 of FF&E over 7 years. The next $14,000 represents the amortization of $210,000 over 15 years.

Would you like $34,000 of tax free income for the next 7 years? That would certainly help pay the note to the seller.

Finally, in some cases an asset sale benefits the seller as well. For example, if there are a few minority shareholders of the seller corporation that don't want to sell, a majority of the shares can still affect an asset sale. The shareholders who don't want to sell can make the seller corporation jump through some hoops, but can't prevent the sale.

That isn't the case with a stock purchase. In the absence of a buy-sell contract, the shareholder can refuse to sell his shares. The shares are the property of the shareholder and the corporation cannot force a sale.

Why a Stock Sale?
So why would any buyer agree to a stock purchase?

First, if there are contracts or licenses that make up a big part of the business purchase, the business sale can often be made without notifying the other party of licensor (although many contracts and licenses today contain "change in control" provisions that require notice or approval if a majority interest in the corporation is transferred).

Second, if the seller demands a stock sale and is unwilling to consider an asset sale. Then, if the buyer wants the business badly enough, she'll have to buy the stock to make it happen.

But, as you can see from the example above, a stock purchase can be quite costly for the buyer.

Luckily, today most sellers recognize that small businesses are sold through asset purchases and are ready to make the sale on that basis.

Detailed Investigation.

Once an offer is made and accepted either through a contract or a letter of intent, you'll begin your detailed investigation (or "due diligence review") of the business.

If you've ever bought a home, you know how important it is to inspect the roof, the structural components – walls, foundation, etc., the appliances, heating and air conditioning, electric and plumbing systems.

Before you spend that much money and obligate yourself to that mortgage – the largest investment most people make prior to buying a business - you want to be sure everything is just as the seller says it is.

Likewise, you must also examine the business you're thinking about buying. Examining a business, though, is more detailed. And it requires financial, legal and general business expertise.

Most buyers know they have to review all the financial records. A few even know that they need to look at the lease.

The biggest mistake I see with due diligence, though, is trying to do it alone. Next is failing to do an in-depth investigation.

A Lease Time Bomb.

A few years ago I reviewed a lease as part of a due diligence review. As any business owner will tell you, next to salaries, rent is probably the biggest expense of a small business.

The buyer, my client, had reviewed the lease before me and, as he gave it to me, said: "It seems to be in order." The lease had been entered by the seller during the last recession and was for five years with a five-year renewal option. The lease rate was extremely favorable and only increased at 3.5% annually.

Those paragraphs were, in fact, typical. However, buried deep in the transfer provisions of the lease was an "option" giving the landlord the right to adjust the rent to a "market rate" if there was a transfer of the lease.

Based on this provision, the lease rate could have gone up by more than 15%, which would have had a big negative effect on the adjusted net of the business.

Because the value of the business is based on the money it makes and any increase in the rent would have greatly reduced the net for the business, my client would be paying way too much for the business if the rent adjusted.

Since it was only an option for the landlord and we were within the due diligence period, we notified the seller of the problem and the parties agreed to freeze the due diligence period. Then, the seller contacted the landlord to try to resolve the issue.

Now this is certainly not a position you want to be in. You think you've sold the business at a good price only to find out your landlord had planted a landmine in the lease. This landmine could have torpedoed the whole deal.

Ultimately, the landlord agreed (in writing, of course) to an adjustment ahead of the sale. So, my client and the seller agreed to reduce the selling price to reflect the additional expense and lower net profit.

Had the seller had his attorney review the lease before he signed it, he'd have received the full purchase price.

But this clearly exemplifies the need for expert help.

Now, to be sure, most people could do what lawyers and accountants do. It isn't rocket science.

In fact, I'm sure that I could do what you do for a living. All I have to do is go through the schooling and training you went through, then work in the industry for a few years.

All anyone has to do to learn a skill and become proficient is to devote a bunch of attention and time. According to a Harvard Business Review article, it takes 10,000 hours of work in a particular area to become an expert. And that time can't be condensed. So, it's best to tap into another's experience.

It's that experience that enables lawyers and accountants to see contracts and financial statements with different eyes than lay people.

Expect Poor Financial Records.

Due diligence review of small business financial records is particularly tricky. Most small business financial records aren't prepared with the same expertise as a larger business.

Another client of mine hired an accountant to review a small business' financial statements. He wanted to know how much the business actually made.

The financial records were a mess (and this isn't uncommon). Things didn't match up and personal transactions were mixed with business transaction (a definite problem on many fronts).

After reconstructing the financial statements from the checks and receipts, the CPA determined that the owner benefit wasn't close to the seller's claims. As a result, the purchase price was reduced by much more than the accountant's fee.

Now, I don't think the seller was trying to pull a fast one. Rather, he just didn't know because he had no clue about financial record keeping.

The goal, though, for any due diligence investigation is to know where the warts are. There are no perfect businesses. They all have problems. (By the way, if you're holding out for a perfect business, you'll waste a lot of time and money.)

You just want to know how imperfect is the business you're interested in buying. Of course, you have to know how things should be in order to know when they aren't right.

Most people will look at what is there to see if it "looks good." But, it is sometimes more important to know what should be there that isn't.

When performing a due diligence review of the business, you should have a comprehensive list of documents to request from the seller. Sellers usually will not have all of the documents. But, by requesting them and having the seller indicate (preferably in writing) what isn't there, you're getting information about the business.

If, by way of example, the seller tells you there is no written lease for the property, you now know there is a risk that you'll have to move in as little as 15 days should the landlord decide he wants the space back. This would compel you to add a contingency (condition) to your purchase contract that the landlord and you agree to a lease of, perhaps, 3 years.

While that might seem obvious, there are clearly others that are missed all the time such as supplier contracts, employee non-compete agreements and customer contracts.

Documents to Consider Reviewing.

The following are some documents, agreements and instruments you may want to request from the seller and, in certain cases, have reviewed by your attorney or accountant. Reviewing them without understanding what is in the documents and what should be in the documents is useless.

Corporate / LLC Related Documents.

- Articles of Incorporation / Articles of Organization and all amendments.
- By-Laws and shareholders agreement or LLC operating agreement.
- Minutes of Board of Director or Manager Meetings.
- Minutes of shareholder or member meetings (Annual and Special).
- Merger Agreements.
- Copies of Share Certificates and List of shareholders or members.
- Stock purchase agreements .
- Asset purchase agreements.
- Notes made by or to the company to or from any shareholder or member.
- Agreements between the company and its shareholder or members.
- Qualifications to do business in any state.
- Annual and other reports and information filed by the company with the Secretary of State from the time of its inception.

- Other corporate documents pertaining to the company or LLC.

Contracts and Agreements.

- Contracts between the company (or any shareholder or member) and third parties, including, vendors, service providers, licensors, licensees, banks, employees and customers.
- Loan agreements, notes and security agreements made or entered by the company.

Financial Statements.

- Tax Returns: federal, state, sales and tangible property for the past three (3) fiscal years.
- Asset list and depreciation schedule.
- Balance Sheet for the past three (3) fiscal year end dates and as of the date of your request, including detailed accounts payable and accounts receivable.
- Profit and Loss Statements for the past three (3) fiscal years and as of the date of your request.
- Corporate bank account statements for the past three (3) fiscal years.
- Purchase orders and inventory records for the past three (3) fiscal years.
- Real Property and other tax statements for the past three (3) fiscal years.
- Notices of Audit and all correspondence with taxing authorities and governmental agencies.

Asset Lists.
- Inventory list.
- Equipment and other tangible assets (e.g., FFE) list.
- Intellectual property list (e.g., trademarks, software licenses, patents, trade secrets, customer lists).
- Depreciation Schedules.
- Lists of, and documentation for, all liens and encumbrances against any assets of the company.
- Equipment and Vehicle leases.
- Equipment and Vehicle Maintenance Histories.

Employee Matters.
- Documentation for all employee benefit plans maintained by the company, including, but not limited to: health insurance plans; pension plans; profit sharing plans; and incentive stock option plans.
- List of employees and compensation rates and amounts.
- Current employee handbook.
- A list of all employees who were terminated or voluntarily left the company in the last twelve months, together with the basis for dismissal, if applicable.
- A list of all claims whether written or verbal made by employees against the company in the past three years.

- All sub-contractor agreements, written and verbal, including, for verbal agreements a complete description of the arrangement.

Litigation.
- Copies of all pleadings and orders for any lawsuit in which the company or company's shareholder or member is or was a party.
- A list of all demands (verbal and written) made by third parties against the company or company's shareholder or member for compensation or actions.

Real Property.
- Copies of all leases and subleases for all real property used by the company.
- Copies of all contracts other than leases and subleases relating to any interest in real property held by the company.
- Copies of the deeds for all Real property owned by the company.
- All environmental reports, audits or reviews pertaining to any real property owned or leased by company at any time.
- List of all hazardous materials purchased, used or disposed of by company.

Miscellaneous
- All business plans for the company developed over the past three (3) years

- All other documents that relate to any material aspect of the business of the company, the assets of the company, the future prospects of the company or the officers, directors and employees of the company

<u>Sales Tax</u>.

Sales tax, in particular, is a thorny issue. A statute in Florida (and many other states) makes a buyer liable for the sales taxes that a seller did not pay – even when the sale is accomplished via an asset purchase. This law requires the buyer to hold back some money in case there is a sales tax liability.

Normally, this would be addressed in the due diligence review. You'd check with the state to see if the taxes had been paid.

Unfortunately, the taxing authorities don't work that fast. If you request an audit of the seller's records by the state (which is required to get an "all clear" from the state), it can take six to eight weeks or more. So, most buyers don't go this route.

If there is seller financing in the deal, this can be dealt with by providing a right of setoff in the seller note and by making sure the note is sufficient in amount and payment term. When the state shows up with a tax deficiency, the buyer makes a claim on the seller. If the seller doesn't pay, the payments that would normally go to the note are then paid to the state.

This also presents problems, however. Normally, the buyer will have to pay the state in one lump sum. Yet the note is paid in relatively small installments. The buyer may, therefore, have to come up with cash in excess of the note payments in order to pay the state.

This is another reason to have an accountant help you with your due diligence review of the business financial records. She'll be able to see if there is a mismatch between the inventory purchased for sale and the declared sales for sales tax returns. It isn't always fool proof, but its better than not looking or doing it yourself.

Finally, if the seller talks about taking cash out of the business (and many of them do), he's admitting to you that he isn't paying taxes (sales or income) on that money. So, you know there's a problem and its just a matter of whether the government finds out about it before it becomes your problem.

The state does register tax liens once they get around to deciding sales taxes haven't been paid. Liens and encumbrances like this are described below.

Liens and Encumbrances.
Over the years I've seen many instances when a buyer purchases a business only to find out that some third party has a claim on the assets of that business. This claim is known as a lien or encumbrance (both of which I will call a lien).

If you buy a business (or its assets) that are subject to a lien, you could have to pay off the lien yourself in order to keep them. That means you might pay twice? And, though you might be able to sue the seller for that money, you still have to come up with the money to pay the lien holder and an attorney out of your pocket.

As I'm sure you can imagine, finding out that you don't really own what you just paid for can be quite a shock.

A lien is a "cloud" on your ownership of some or all of the assets of the business. This means that someone else has the right to legally take your business assets and sell them to satisfy the seller's debts.

Therefore, you have to make sure there are no liens on the business you're buying. And, if there are any, they have to be satisfied or paid at the time you close the purchase.

Liens usually come from any of three situations:
- A loan where the business assets is pledged as security.
- Unpaid taxes.
- A court judgment.

For most liens the law says that purchasers "without knowledge of the lien" who pay good money for a business are protected from the lien holder making a claim on the business assets.

But, don't get comfortable just yet. What the law gives with the right hand, it takes with the left; the key is the term "without knowledge of the lien."

This doesn't mean the lien holder actually sends you a letter notifying you that there is a lien. Instead, the law lets lien holders put the world on notice of their lien by filing documents with the state or someone designated by the state. This is referred to as "constructive notice."

So, if a bank loaned money to a business and took a security interest against its assets, it will file a UCC-1 in the public records to put everyone on notice of the security interest. In theory, this will put all buyers on notice so they can make sure the bank is paid and its security interest is released. The bank's lien stays on the public records for a set amount of time (usually 5 years) unless it's renewed or paid off.

Likewise, with a judgment, the judgment creditor records the judgment and, depending on the law of the particular state, files it with the state to put everyone else on notice.

Unfortunately for buyers, thought, there are special rules for governments (you probably could have guessed this). So, in some cases, even if you search the public records, you might not know that a lien exists.

This situation is often the case with sales tax payments. The state taxing agency may only discover months after the seller has filed its return, that it underpaid the taxes due (not to mention the problem that can arise if the seller isn't remitting taxes it collects on all sales). Then, when it does figure it out, the delinquency notices come to the buyer at the business location.

That problem cannot easily be solved. To protect yourself as much as possible, you must have provisions in your purchase contract and, in my opinion, some seller financing. The contract should require the seller to represent to you that all taxes have been paid, in full, and should give you the right to make a claim against the seller (also known as "indemnification"). The seller financing will give you a place to get that money from.

Unfortunately, protection is not the complete answer.

Tax liens present the biggest problem. First, the taxing authority can begin to collect the lien at any time. In some cases this means you could show up to open your shop one day, only to find the doors padlocked with a notice. Not only do you have to rush to the tax collector's office with check in hand, your customers are now going to wonder about your business practices – the business goodwill you just paid for may be worth a lot less now.

Second, a tax lien raises a red flag on the way the seller kept the books and records of the business. It means you should delve much deeper into the business to find the other warts. These warts probably include other improperly filed tax returns that could come back to haunt you after you buy the business.

If there is a lien, you'll have to pay a lien holder in cash immediately to have it satisfied. Since, most seller financing permits you to make payments over a number of years, you may find yourself having to come up with more cash than you thought you would (or than you had).

For example, if there is an undisclosed $15,000 tax lien and the state wants to take action to collect that lien, you'll have to come up with $15,000 plus interest on the lien, in cash. If you had seller financing that required monthly payments of $1,300.00, it will take just shy of a year's worth of payments to make up the principal amount of the lien.

It would be like having to come up with a year's payment in advance. And, of course, if you had the money in the first place, you would use it to grow the business, not pay the seller's debts!

Now the situation could be far worse. But, as you can see, even a small lien will create a cash flow problem for you. Therefore, it is best to avoid this situation all together.

To determine if any liens exist, a search of the public records is conducted. Today, this is done through the Internet, although there are services that can be used to do a more thorough search. These services may be used on a case-by-case basis, such as in the case of bank financing.

A search via the Internet is accomplished by searching the public records websites for:
- UCC-1 filings;
- Judgment Liens;
- Tax Liens (federal and state);
- Local government taxes (e.g., tangible property taxes); and
- Pending lawsuits (usually in the county where the business is located).

If a lien exists, your attorney will usually try to get the pay off amount from the creditor in the form of a letter, stating the amount due as of a certain date.

Then, at closing, some of the proceeds from the sale (money that would otherwise be due the seller) are used by your attorney to pay off the creditor. The attorney should always be the one to pay the creditor from the sale proceeds because you will have a record that the lien has been paid and the creditor will usually send the release to the attorney for filing.

In some purchases I've been involved in the seller will say they've paid the lien just before closing, but didn't have the creditor's release. This situation should be avoided at all costs. The only thing to do is to have the attorney hold the amount due on the lien in escrow until the seller can provide a satisfaction.

According to laws in most states, if the creditor is paid but fails to provide a satisfaction of the lien, the creditor can be subject to sanction.

Sometimes the seller wants to negotiate the amount due the creditor or they'll claim the creditor pay off amount is incorrect.

First, know that this is a risky situation. If you need this creditor to continue to run the business, the seller's attempt to negotiate the debt could create bad will and the creditor may refuse to do business with you. Also, the creditor could take action to foreclose the lien – that is, take the business assets.

And, if you have bank financing, the bank usually will not permit seller to do this. The bank wants to ensure its lien is in first place – that is, the bank gets paid first.

Second, if you're willing to give the seller a shot at cutting the debt, you have to set a time limit. In my opinion, this should be sixty or ninety days after closing, but, never more than six months.

Third, the full amount due plus the interest that will accrue during the time the seller attempts to negotiate the debt (plus a week or two) should be held in trust by your attorney. The attorney should be able to pay the lien automatically (i.e., without the seller's consent) after the time period is up or if the creditor takes any action to collect on the lien.

Finally, you should be able to set off all of the expenses you incur as a result of these actions against the seller financing.

Searching for and paying off liens and encumbrances of the seller will ensure that you own the business you just bought and no one will show up on your doorstep one day, demanding a check.

The Purchase and Sale Contract.

As discussed previously, the purchase contract must hold the seller to all of his statements about the business and his post-purchase promises. Everything that you and the seller have discussed must be written in the contract for it to be applicable.

Chapter One describes many general contract issues that are applicable to a business purchase. There are some particular nuances to business purchase contracts.

An asset purchase agreement will generally be structured with a number of sections:
- Description of the deal, including purchase price and any seller financing.
- Description of assets purchase and liabilities assumed, if any.

- Representations and warranties (promises) of the seller about the seller, the business, its assets, its relationships with landlords, governments, vendors, employees, its disputes with third parties and any other important matters.
- Representations and warranties of the buyer (usually much less than are provided by the seller).
- Documents, agreements and instruments to be executed and delivered at closing, such as non-compete agreements, notes, security agreements, lease assignments, debt and contract assumption agreements, affidavits, and any others that are related to your deal. These documents are usually attached as exhibits to the agreement.
- Pre closing covenants (things that are to happen before the closing) such as seller securing landlord approval, due diligence review, the buyer getting financing to close the deal, and other matters.
- Post closing covenants (things that are to happen after the closing) such as, the seller's shareholder staying on to work in the business for some period of time, or the seller working to transition customers to the buyer.
- How the buyer or seller can get out of the deal without closing. This is important where a landlord would have to approve a lease transfer or there are some contingencies that have to be resolved.
- Indemnification. Creating the line in the sand so that the seller is responsible for things that happened before the closing and the buyer is responsible for things that happen after the closing.
- "Boilerplate" provisions that deal with things that have to be dealt with in all contracts, but that must be tailored to your circumstances.

The overall purpose of the contract is to give a clear picture of the state of the business, what the parties have agreed to do before, at and after the closing, and to allocate risk between the buyer and the seller.

Also, the seller's and buyer's shareholders are generally parties to asset purchase agreements. For the buyer this means that, once the money is paid to the seller's shareholders and the selling corporation dissolved, the buyer can look directly to the seller's shareholders for any breaches of the agreements. This is absolutely critical and you should not, in the vast majority of situations, buy a business where the seller's shareholders refuse to sign the contract individually.

Secure Third Party Approvals and Close.
Once the landlord has consented to transfer the lease and other open issues are completed, the parties meet to close the transaction. Closing should be a ministerial matter – signing documents and delivering checks. After the closing, you're the new owner and the real work begins.

Chapter Ten

Exit Planning Mistakes

If you're like most owners, your business is your largest financial asset. You've worked hard to grow it. You've seen it through good times and bad. You're a successful entrepreneur.

Yet, you're looking to make a change. Maybe it's not that much fun anymore. Or, maybe you're focused too much on the day-to-day issues rather than growth and big picture things. You'd like to take some time off to relax before your next venture. Or, perhaps you're looking to cash out and retire.

According to the New York Times Bestseller, Millionaire Next Door, by Thomas Stanley, most millionaires became millionaires through their small businesses.

But, moving from successful business owner to cash-in-the-bank requires that you successfully sell your business.

Plus: only <u>one in five businesses that are put up for sale actually sell</u>! (That's not a typo – only 1 in 5.)

Cashing out of your business means finding the right buyer, at the right price and making sure you get paid.

There are big risks when you decide to cash-out.
- Will you leave money on the table because you didn't market the business properly?
- Will you destroy value you built in the business?
- Will your customers, vendors, employees and competitors learn the business is for sale?
- What's the 'right' price?
- Who will you sell to?
- Is it the right time to sell?
- What can you do to improve the business for a higher price?
- Will the proceeds from the sale be enough to support your retirement?

Bottom line: you want to get maximum price in the shortest time with the least hassle.

The first mistake that entrepreneurs make when it comes to exit planning is not planning.

You'll usually sell only one business in your lifetime. So, you only get one chance to get it right. The way to be sure you're business is one of the 20% that sell is to plan the process of the sale at least two to five years before you sell.

Improperly Pricing Your Business.

After failing to plan, pricing your business is one of the most important aspects of selling it and an area where most business owners make big mistakes.

You've got to price it right to make sure you're not leaving money on the table.

Of course, setting your price too low means leaving money on the table.

This is an easy problem to fix, right? If you think it's too low, just raise the price.

Ah, but how do you know if its too high?

In fact, setting your price too high is a bigger problem that setting it too low. Why?

Well, first, it means you'll own the business for a lot longer than you'd like. With an overpriced business you'll cut out the "real" buyers.

Our culture in the United States doesn't like to bargain. For the most part, we view a price as "the" price and we won't bargain if it's too high. We'll just walk away to the next deal.

Think about it. Are most of your friends comfortable buying a car? Do they like visiting the dealer to "negotiate" over price and terms? Do they feel comfortable sitting with the dealer's finance manger?

In fact, Americans are so much against bargaining that some auto dealers have developed "no haggle" pricing as point of differentiation.

Now you have to add to this cultural mindset the buyer's fear. For most buyers this is their first business purchase. And they're terrified. If they get a hint that the business is overpriced, they'll bail. In fact, they're looking for any reason not to move forward.

This means that, if you set the price for your business too high, you won't get many (if any offers). People won't even say they're not interested; they'll come up with excuses or just walk off into the sunset doing nothing.

They might think you're unrealistic and conclude there's no reason to try to make an offer. Or they might not want to insult you. But, either way, you're not getting offers.

And, those few that do make an offer will usually low ball it. They're the few bold buyers who aren't afraid to make any offer. They're looking for deals and know you're overpriced. So, they figure "why not try; there's nothing to lose."

Worse than the bargain hunters, though, is what will happen to your psyche as time goes on.

Every owner starts out excited at the prospect of selling, waiting for the offers to come in. In fact, once you decide to sell your business, it's sold in your mind; you just have to sign the documents.

But, as time goes by, the owner of the overpriced business starts to feel uneasy.

As weeks and weeks go by without any offers (and often without any showings) they become very concerned; some even begin to panic.

Think of it this way: imagine that one day your business phone stops ringing and customers stop coming in your door. This goes on for days. Then a week. Then a few weeks. Then months. What would go through your mind? What would you do?

That feeling is even worse when you're trying to sell your biggest financial asset. You've got plans. You've made up your mind to move on. The sale is only a formality to your new life.

You're panicked. So, when a low ball or goofy offer eventually comes in, you're more likely to take it. And then you're really leaving money on the table.

To avoid this problem you'll have to know how to properly price the business; you've got to understand small business value.

I must tell you that, sadly, there are a lot of professional advisors who either don't know how to price your business or they won't take the time to do it right.

Not too long ago this happened to Sally and Bob. They had operated their small business (literally a "mom and pop" store) for the past ten years after Bob got early retirement from a large corporation. They decided that it was time for a real retirement and contacted another broker in town. He listed their business for $500,000.

It sat. And sat. And sat.

After 6 months with absolutely no traffic, Sally and Bob contacted the broker to lower the price (notice I didn't say the broker contacted them).

So they dropped the price to $450,000.

Then, it sat. And sat. And sat some more.

When the listing agreement expired they came to my firm.

After we'd done a comprehensive valuation, we had some good news and some bad news for Sally and Bob.

Using the method I describe in Appendix D, we determined there was no way they were going to sell for $450,000. Or even $400,000. The most their business was worth was $300,000.

They were actually relieved. They told us that at first they wondered what the problem was. That wonder turned to fear that they'd never be able to sell. After we talked, I sensed that the fear turned to anger at the first broker.

Unfortunately, some business brokers follow the path of least resistance. Rather than educate business owners about the true value of the business, they list at any price the owner requests.

Why? Because listings generate buyer inquiries. Most prospective buyers, who call on a particular business, never buy that business anyway. So, these brokers use your listing just to generate traffic for their brokerage firm. If they're not selling your business to the buyer who called, they'll sell another.

It's not a problem for the broker, just you.

Meanwhile, you sit and become more concerned like Sally and Bob.

See Appendix D for detailed information about business value.

Failing to Maximize Business Value.

Failing to maximize business value in advance of marketing the business for sale is another critical mistake.

Maximizing the value of your business requires that you know:

- The two – and only two - types of business buyers;
- Which buyers will pay the most for your business and why; and
- How to tailor your business so it meets the needs of those buyers.

There are two types of business buyers: financial buyers and strategic buyers.

Financial Buyers.

Financial buyers purchase businesses based on cash flow. They'll buy a company to get an income and for an opportunity to grow and improve the business for more cash flow.

The value of a business to a financial buyer is a function of how much cash flow the business produces and the risk of how likely that cash flow is to continue or grow in the future.

Strategic Buyers.

Strategic buyers, on the other hand, purchase businesses based on something more than just cash flow. They'll buy a company to get access to a component of the company that can be used to improve the buyer's existing business and for the cash flow it produces. These components can include a customer base, special technology or employee capabilities.

The key for you as a business seller is that, because of the added benefit to the strategic buyer, they'll pay more for your business than an investment buyer. Therefore, making your business appealing to strategic buyers is one key to maximizing its value.

Consider CoolTech Corporation a technology company that wants to sell its product into a new market. It could try to sell directly to that market. But its sales would be limited by the experience and credibility of CoolTech Corporation's sales team in the new market, and by its understanding of the new market's needs and terminology.

If, on the other hand, CoolTech Corporation bought another company (we'll call this one ACME Corporation) that already served the new market, CoolTech Corporation would acquire ACME Corporation's customer base and products or services, as well as an experienced sales force with a reputation and staff experienced in the new market.

ACME Corporation is worth more to CoolTech Corporation because, in addition to the cash flow coming from ACME Corporation's existing operations, CoolTech Corporation can grow its original business by selling more of its current products through ACME Corporation's sales channels, as well as cut costs from duplicated back office operations.

Now CoolTech Corporation can make a business case based on the return from the added sales plus ACME Corporation's cash flow and can, therefore, pay a premium over a straight cash-flow-ROI analysis.

Unfortunately, most businesses are purchased by financial buyers because the business owner hasn't planned the exit in advance, and hasn't considered who could be a strategic buyer or tailored the business for those strategic buyers.

Creating a strategic buyer market for your business requires advance planning.

Consider what companies would likely be strategic buyers for your business. Do you have a particular niche (market, geographic or other) that another industry could exploit with current services or products? Does your business have one or two large direct competitors? What other businesses could benefit from access to your customers, your systems or your technologies?

Once you've identified possible strategic buyers, you must put in place the structure that will maximize the value of your business to those buyers.

First, build a good quality customer base in a well defined niche. Compete only on service or technological expertise. Determine your company's value proposition (which, for a small business should never be lowest price) based on your customer's needs and make sure you create a long lasting relationship so they buy from you again and again.

Then, systematize the business, hire the best employees and pay and incentivize them to view the business as owners, even if they're not. If the business requires you to run it, it will be much less valuable to all buyers. Your key employees are part of your business' value proposition and you should have 'golden handcuffs' keeping them in place.

Finally, watch your profitability constantly. Analyze every decision based on profitability. If you invest in the business, make sure you know when you'll receive cash flow from that investment. Be sure profit will grow.

Of course there are specific things to do for your company, depending on its size, market position and product or service.

Trying to Sell Your Business By Yourself.
If your business is worth $500,000 or more and you weren't an investment banker or business broker in your past life, you shouldn't even think about selling it yourself.

There's a commercial that recently ran on TV that began with a doctor in scrubs standing at a nurses' station in a hospital with a phone to his ear. The doctor is speaking into the phone saying: 'now find the space between the 3rd and 4th ribs and make an incision.'

The camera then cuts to a man in his home also holding a phone to his head. He's in his kitchen, in his other hand is a scalpel with the blade pointed to his bare chest. On his forehead are small beads of sweat; he looks nervous. Haltingly, he moves the scalpel towards his chest, then stops and looks at the phone, clearly confused. After a brief moment of silence, the man says, "Shouldn't you be doing this?"

A narrator breaks in: 'At Smith Jones Financial Advisors we think making your own investment decisions isn't so smart either.'

Of course, the point is you'd better be sure you know what you're doing when it comes to the really important things, like your health and wealth. On-the-job learning when your life or your financial well being are at risk is just plain stupid.

Because your business is probably your largest financial asset, you've got to be careful with that scalpel.

Whatever you do in your business, I'm sure it took you time to become proficient. It took you time to know where the problems show themselves and how to fix them.

According to the recent book *Outliers* and an article in *Harvard Business Review*, it takes about 10,000 hours -

about 5 years of full time work - to become an expert at a trade or profession.

Unless you're an attorney or a transaction advisor, I'm sure you're more proficient at your business than I am. Why? Because you do what you do every working day. And I don't.

On the other hand, I do business deals day-in-and-day-out and have been doing them for more than 16 years. That means I know what to expect because I've experienced it before. This means I plan for the landmines and anticipate the speed bumps before they come up. Plus, I know how to minimize or avoid them.

Because you've probably never done this before (or only did it once in the past), you don't know where the landmines are until you set them off!

It's a lot cheaper to pay for that experience by hiring qualified advisors than it is to suffer the consequences of the inevitable mistakes you'll surely make in the process.

The following are some additional reasons not to go it alone when selling your business.

Confidentiality.
Let's take a look at the difference between selling a business and selling real estate such as your home.

When you decide to sell your home (or any real estate for that matter) you want everyone to know it's for sale. You put up signs, take out ads and hand out flyers.

You want a lot of offers. Having all those people know your house is for sale makes it more likely that you'll get offers and it doesn't hurt the house any.

It's just the opposite for your businesses.

Sure, you want a lot of offers. But, when people know a business is for sale, it actually hurts the business.

Employees wonder what'll happen to their jobs when the business sells. Some will think they should get some of the money because they helped build it. Others will look for new jobs or begin "protecting themselves."

Knowledgeable and trained employees are a critical component to a valuable going concern business. But losing one or two non-key employees isn't a problem. Losing key employees or losing a lot of employees is a big problem.

Your employees are part of the glue that holds the customers – and their money – to your business.

Next, customers will become concerned. What will change? Where they were loyal, they become open to switching to competitors. And, you certainly don't want your competition to find out.

Because your business' value is based on cash flow, the loss of customers will decrease your business' value.

This means that confidentially marketing the business is absolutely essential.

This is accomplished by making prospective buyers sign legally binding confidentiality agreements, by letting you know who they are before we let them know who you are, and by restricting access to information until the general deal terms are agreed upon.

<u>*Objectivity*</u>
This is your baby; you're emotionally involved.

If you have children or, even better, grandchildren, you know what I mean. Your children or grandchildren are, of course, simply the cutest and brightest humans ever to walk the planet. Why? Because they're yours.

It's the same with your business.

You've lived this business. You've felt the pain and joy of building and nurturing it. It's a part of you.

Realistically assessing the business and knowing when you should give, hold or push are things that only a dispassionate advisor can bring to you. You must have a clear vision when you deal with your most valuable asset. You need an experienced advisor to help you get that clear vision.

Taking your eye off the management ball.

Building and running a business is more than a full-time job. Brokering a business is a full-time job. It's unlikely you can do both without one or the other suffering.

There's no worse time for a business to fall back then when you're trying to sell it. Having to explain that to a prospective buyer isn't good. And once you've made the decision to sell, you don't want it to drag on.

Plus, there are a lot of tire-kicker buyers out there. There are a lot of callers who will respond just looking for free information. Dealing with these useless inquiries, will waste a lot of your time.

Someone should perform due diligence on prospective buyers so you don't waste your time on someone with no money or no capability to buyer your business.

Negotiation.

Several months ago I was negotiating a business sale on behalf of a buyer with another attorney in town. This attorney normally represented businesses in court, rather than doing deals. He was a litigator.

I prepared a proposed asset purchase agreement and related documents and sent them to this other attorney. He immediately called me, stating: "There's no way my clients will sign this agreement personally! That's why they have a corporation."

As our conversation continued I tried to explain to him that it was customary to have the shareholders personally bound in the sale of a small business because, once the business was sold, the corporation would be dissolved and the money paid to the shareholders. Also, because the shareholders operated the business day in and day out and were the true beneficiaries of the deal, only they'd know some of the things that were described in the contract.

But, he wouldn't have any of it. So the deal died.

The sellers didn't sell that business on the next offer either again because the attorney didn't know what points to negotiate and what were customary.

Finally the sellers woke up and got a new attorney.

When you're not involved in business sales on a regular basis (even if you have a law degree), you don't know what is normal, what is out of the ordinary and what should be there but is missing. You have to know what you can and should get, and how to advocate for it.

Knowing what you can expect is essential because it protects you from blowing a deal on something that is just not reasonable. That knowledge also protects you from accepting less than you should.

Using a broker who's guilty of "sign everyone up, then bulletin board market."

As described above in the section titled: Failing to Maximize Business Value., the way you market the business will have a direct effect on the ultimate sales price. Certain business brokers will cost you money because of their marketing tactics.

These brokers sign up as many business sellers as possible, no matter what the price or terms the seller demands. They collect listings.

Then they do nothing more than post the listing on the Internet to get buyer calls. In their view the purpose of a listing is to generate calls from prospective buyers.

It's well known in the business brokerage industry that buyers rarely buy the business they first call about. But having the listing gets a prospective buyer to call the listing broker so that broker can "match" that buyer with another listing and get a commission. These brokers sell buyers other agents' listings. And, if one of their listings sells, that's just gravy.

Your business broker / advisor should have a limited number of appropriately priced deals so he can pay attention to your listing. In my opinion, no business broker can properly service 40, 50 or 100 listings? Even if your business is one of the best, that broker can't remember your name, let alone think about who would be a good buyer candidate to market to.

You need a professional experienced business broker who will tell you the truth about your business and actively market it in a way that maximizes its value.

Letting the Buyer find the Business Skeletons in the Closet.

You have to know the problems with your business and you have to disclose them (at the right place and time) to the buyer before he finds them out for himself.

When you properly disclose problems, they seem less problematic and everyone looks for solutions. If, on the other hand, the buyer "discovers" a problem, he's thinking: "What else is here that I haven't found?" No surprise is good in a business sale.

Failing to do "Due Diligence" on the Buyer.

Sellers expect buyers to look behind the curtain when it comes to their business. But many sellers don't investigate the buyer.

The deal isn't done until you're fully paid and you no longer have any liability to the business creditors (e.g., the landlord). What is the buyer's history?

A couple of years ago there were two gentlemen in Central Florida who would buy a business, drain every bit of cash from it, default of the lease and the seller financing, then move on. They did this in the span of a few weeks. Then they'd move on to a different part of the area and do it again.

It was only after a few business brokers and lawyers started discussing the situation that everyone became aware this was a scheme. Had the sellers done a bit of due diligence on these guys, they might have turned up some questionable dealings and raised a few red flags for further review.

You've got to know as much as you can about the buyer to protect your financial future.

Appendix A: Corporation Questions and Answers

A corporation is separate and distinct from its owners, who are known as shareholders or stockholders. A corporation can enter contracts, sue and be sued. It is, literally, an artificial entity that has rights and obligations that are different from the rights and obligations of its shareholders.

There are three key groups of people involved in a corporation: shareholders, directors and officers.

Shareholders.
Shareholders are the owners of the corporation. Each shareholder has rights to do or get some or all of the following:

- Receive dividends and distributions (profits).
- Vote for directors.
- Receive the assets left over after the corporation is liquidated.

Shareholders can also have other rights and things known as preferences. Preferences give one group of shareholders the ability to get ahead of other shareholders when things happen. This might happen when the corporation is dissolved and one group of shareholders gets their money out before another group. These preferences are written into the articles of incorporation and apply to classes and series of stock.

Different "classes" and "series" of stock and the rights of each shareholder who owns that stock are described, exactly, in the articles of incorporation.

There can be one shareholder, a few shareholders, or thousands or millions of shareholders.

Directors.

Directors are the people who make "policy" decisions for the corporation. These are decisions about what business the corporation is in and other high level decisions. Directors are elected by the shareholders (at the annual shareholder meeting) to serve terms typically between 1 and 3 years.

Usually there are between 1 and 9 directors that make up the Board of Directors of the corporation. Any more than 9 members and the Board of Directors becomes too large to be effective.

The Board of Directors has regular meetings to review the business of the corporation, financial results and to make important business decisions. The Board of Directors also elects the officers of the corporation.

Officers.

The officers of the corporation manage the day-to-day business of the corporation.

Officers can include a president, vice-presidents, secretary, treasurer, chief executive officer (CEO), chief operating officer (COO) and any other title the bylaws provide.

No particular officers are required to be appointed by the Board of Directors of a Florida corporation. But, because the corporation can only act through the officers, there needs to be at least one for the corporation to be able to operate its business.

Each officer has the responsibilities described in the bylaws. Most often, the secretary keeps the record books of the corporation and of the meetings of the Board of Directors and shareholders, and the treasurer is responsible for the corporation's accounts. And, the president or chief executive officer is the highest ranking officer in the corporation and reports to the Board of Directors.

In small business corporations (sometimes referred to as "closely held" or "close" corporations), a few people (or one) may fill all of the roles. One, two or three people could be the sole shareholders, directors, officers and employees of the corporation. This is entirely permissible and doesn't result in a loss of the limited liability benefit.

And, as discussed above, because management (officers and directors) is separated from ownership (stockholders), a corporation can have "investor" shareholders who do not take part in the daily operation of the business, but benefit from the increase in value of the corporation's business and properties.

Formation.

Forming a corporation begins with the filing of articles of incorporation with the secretary of state by an incorporator. The incorporator, the person who forms the corporation, signs the articles of incorporation and files them (usually through an attorney).

In Florida, the filing fee for the articles and statement identifying the registered agent is $70.00.

Once the articles are filed, the corporation is technically formed. But, if you do nothing more, its like building a house and forgetting to put up interior walls. You're sealed against the outside, but it isn't a great place to live.

It is therefore, important to completely form the corporation by:

- Have an initial meeting of the board of directors.
- Transfer assets to the corporation.
- Adopt bylaws.
- Enter a shareholders / buy-sell agreement.
- Issue stock.
- Filing the appropriate tax forms with the IRS and Florida Department of Revenue.

Frankly it's surprising to me how often these steps aren't done properly.

In one case a person (lets call him Tim) invested approximately $100,000.00 in a corporation. The incorporator, sole officer and sole director, Jack, Tim's "friend," told Tim that Jack's trucking business, including the trucks and trailers, had been transferred to the corporation.

Tim did some analysis of the trucks and decided that his investment was less than the value of the trucks. So, even if things didn't work out, Tim figured he'd get his investment from the sale of the trucks and trailers.

Things didn't work out.

Only when Tim wanted to sell the trucks to get his investment out did Tim find out that the trucks were still owned by Jack personally. Because Jack was in debt up to his eyeballs and was behind on his payments to the bank and other creditors, Jack couldn't sell the trucks and give any money to Tim.

Tim lost his entire investment because the proper paperwork hadn't been fully completed.

A similar scenario is played out when stock isn't properly issued.

Without share certificates and proper board of directors actions, the shareholders can fight over the number of shares and percentages that they should properly own. Sometimes, it isn't until years later that they realize the numbers are incorrect.

What are the ongoing costs of a corporation?

In Florida there is an annual corporate fee of $150.00, if paid on or before May 1 of each year. In addition to the fee, you'll have accountant's fees for preparation of the corporate tax return, costs of a bank account and attorney's fees for the annual corporate housekeeping. Those costs will depend on the activities of the corporation.

Delaware and Nevada Corporations?

If you form a Delaware corporation because the laws are "favorable" or a Nevada corporation for privacy or tax benefit, you're making a huge mistake.

Most small business should create corporations in the state where they're based. This is because a "foreign" corporation – one from a state outside your home state – must be authorized to do business in your home state. To be authorized it must file papers with the state and pay filing fees. Usually, those fees are as much as the fees to form a corporation. Therefore, you **pay twice** to form the same corporation.

Now, you might ask why, are publicly held corporations usually Delaware corporations? And why do some people suggest Nevada corporations?

Delaware's corporate laws tend to favor "management" (the board of directors) and enable the board to more effectively control the corporation. This isn't important to you as a small business owner because you usually already have control. If you're the only shareholder, you have complete control. If you're one of a few shareholders, you should have a shareholders' agreement to control management of the corporation.

Nevada corporations are touted for their secrecy provisions and tax protection. It's my opinion that you should go offshore if you want secrecy. Further, secrecy with a Nevada corporation is usually a myth for small business owners. Unless you'll have an agent who'll act by and for the corporation, someone is going to know you're an employee, officer or director. They'll probably assume you're a shareholder as well.

As far as the tax issue goes, in Florida there is no state income tax on "S" corporations or their shareholders. So, the effect is the same.

In other states, however, if the corporation owns property in the state or does business from the state, it must pay taxes on that portion of its income that comes from the state. So, if you have a Nevada corporation that owns a retail shop or service business in New York, the corporation must register as a foreign corporation in New York and must pay taxes in New York – no tax savings.*

---

* Remember, hoping not to get audited (i.e., caught) is not a tax planning strategy. It's hope.

Appendix B: Limited Liability Company Questions and Answers

A limited liability company (an "LLC") is a business entity that is a cross between a partnership and a corporation. It provides the liability protection that the owners of a corporation receive with the close business relationship that would normally exist in a general partnership. Unlike a corporation, the owner of the LLC – known as a "member" – typically has both ownership and management rights.

Limited liability companies are extremely flexible and offer the ability to vary the arrangement between the owners in a myriad of ways as well as to choose from up to 4 different tax structures. Of course, limitations exist and all options are not available to every LLC.

Limited liability companies provide liability protection that is exactly the same as a corporation, with the close business relationship of a general partnership. So, the LLC is often appropriate for closely held businesses or where the entity will hold real estate. An LLC can also be used for subsidiaries within a larger business.

Members manage the LLC business and receive LLC profits. The members can also elect to have the LLC managed by "managers." Managers are a cross between officers and directors from the corporation.

An LLC is usually not used when there are to be outside investors or key employees are to receive options to buy into the business.

Like a corporation, an LLC is separate and distinct from its owners. It can enter contracts and sue and be sued without involving its owners.

Unlike a corporation, all aspects of the ownership interest of an LLC (a membership interest) are usually not freely transferable. A member may transfer his or her economic interest (e.g., the right to receive profits) at will. But, members usually have to get permission of the other members before a transferee can participate in the management of the LLC business.

And all of the other members have to agree if a member wants to withdraw from the LLC. This often comes as a shock to members who want to "walk away" from a business.

Is the limited liability company a new form of business?
No. In Florida the LLC has been available since 1982. Unfortunately, tax issues often kept people from using an LLC. Until 1998 the LLC had a Florida income tax of approximately 5% of net income. Since that was changed, though, the LLC has become a very popular form of business and investment entity.

Members and Managers

The owners of the LLC are called its members. Members typically have the right to manage the business of the LLC, receive a share of LLC profits (through their capital account) and receive any assets left over after the LLC business has been wound up and liquidated. Membership can be divided into different classes with various rights and preferences.

The members can also elect to have the LLC business managed by "managers" who are elected by the members. The managers manage the day-to-day business of the LLC. Often, managers are given titles that are similar to the officers of a corporation (e.g., President). No managers are required.

It is possible to have a single member LLC without loss of liability protection. For this reason and the tax issues (discussed below), most, if not all, sole proprietors should transfer their businesses to an LLC.

How is a LLC created?

Forming a LLC begins with the filing of articles of organization, signed by a member or the member's authorized representative, with the secretary of state by an incorporator. In Florida, the filing fee for the articles of organization and statement identifying the registered agent is $125.00.

Once the articles are filed, the LLC is formed. The members should then enter an operating agreement that addresses allocation of profits, transfers of membership interests, and other key elements of the management and operation of an LLC.

Does a LLC issue stock certificates?

No. Since the LLC does not have stock, no stock certificates are issued. Sometimes, an LLC issues membership certificates. But, these are not required.

Can creditors easily "pierce" an LLC to hold members personally liable?

No. In Florida, a statute provides that the same rules that apply to corporations and the liability of corporate shareholders also applies to members of an LLC (Section 608.701, Florida Statutes). Therefore, there is no difference.

Delaware and Nevada LLC's?

See the section entitled "Delaware and Nevada Corporations?" in Appendix A.

Appendix C: Basic Taxation of Business Entities

One of the biggest mistakes I see repeatedly is not considering the tax issues that come along with using a corporation or LLC.

It's important to remember that a corporation, and sometimes an LLC, are treated as separate for the owners for tax purposes. Therefore, stock and assets (such as money) can just be transferred between a corporation (or LLC) and its owners.

There are three ways that business entities are taxed:
- Disregarded Tax Status.
- Pass Through Taxation.
- Entity Taxation.

Disregarded Tax Status

Disregarded Tax Status is exactly what it sounds like. The entity is ignored for tax purposes and all of the income and expenses are transferred directly to the owner.

The only entity where this is applicable is a single member limited liability company (unless the owner – member – does something to select a different tax status).

For an LLC owned by an individual, the individual files his taxes as though he was a sole proprietor, but gets the liability protection of the LLC.

Because of this, it is almost always a mistake for anyone to operate as a sole proprietor.

Pass Through Taxation.
There are two forms of pass through taxation: "S" corporation taxation and partnership taxation. They are somewhat similar with several important differences. One of these concerns profit distributions to owners who are active in the business. With a partnership those distributions are earned income and subject to FICA and Medicare taxes. With an "S" corporation status, they're not.

Therefore, the rule of thumb is that, between the two, an operating business (as opposed to a holding company, for example) should elect "S" corporation tax status.

"S" Corporation Tax Status.
The election to be taxed as an "S" corporation is made by filing IRS Form 2553 with the IRS. Once that is properly completed, the corporation (or LLC) is taxed as a "pass through" entity. That means the "S" corporation almost never pays taxes itself.

Instead, the "S" corporation files its tax return (on IRS Form 1120S) with the IRS and issues all of the shareholders K-1 statements. The corporation usually doesn't pay any tax to the IRS. Instead, the K-1 statement shows the shareholders portion of the net income of the corporation for which that shareholder will be taxed.

For example, if a shareholder owns 25% of the issued and outstanding stock of an "S" corporation and the corporation's total net income for the year is $200,000, then that shareholder's K-1 statement will show $50,000 of income allocated to that shareholder. In this way the corporation's income "passes through" to its shareholders.

It's important to note that the income passes to the shareholders whether or not any of them actually get the cash from the corporation. In other words, the K-1 doesn't necessarily come with a check.

Instead, the allocated income is phantom or imputed income to the shareholder. The income is recognized by the IRS, but it is unlikely that the shareholder received it.

Why? Well, the net profit of a corporation will almost never be present in the corporation's bank account at the end of the year. Instead, that money is used to continue or grow the business operations.

As a result, the corporation may not have the funds to pay the shareholders any amount. Furthermore, the corporation isn't actually required to distribute any of the profits to the shareholders.

The benefit of this arrangement is that only the shareholders pay taxes on the corporate income. This reduces the maximum tax rate to approximately 28% to 31%, saving at least 10% of net income from taxes that would have to be paid in an entity tax status double taxation situation. For most people (who are in the 28% tax bracket), the savings will be greater.

The big drawback with an "S" corporation is that the shareholders have to include their share of the corporate income on their tax returns and pay tax on that money. If the corporation distributes cash to the shareholders, this may not be a problem.

But, there are instances when a corporation may not distribute its cash to the shareholders. First, cash and net income (or profit) are quite different. The corporation may have a net income, but not have the cash in its bank account. Or, if the corporation is controlled by other shareholders, it may decide not to distribute cash to its shareholders.

However, even if the shareholder never receives any money from the corporation, he must pay the tax on his share of the corporation's net income. The shareholder could have to pay those taxes by dipping into savings or selling other assets.

Of course, if the corporation has losses, the shareholder may be able to offset those losses against other income. The shareholder must, however, have "basis" in the shares of the corporation in order to do this.

"Basis" is, essentially, an investment in the shares of the corporation (or membership interest of the LLC).

For example, if shareholder A invests $100,000 in ACME Corporation for 75% of the stock and ACME has losses of $100,000 in the first year, shareholder A will be able to deduct $75,000 of those losses against other income he may have. If it has another $100,000 loss in year 2, then shareholder A can only deduct $25,000 against other income because he only has $25,000 of basis left, after deducting the $75,000 in year 1.

Entity Taxation

Entity taxation is commonly referred to as being taxed as a "C" corporation.

A "C" corporation itself pays taxes on its net income. It files form 1120 with the IRS (as its tax return) and pays federal (and possibly state) taxes based on its net income. The maximum corporate rate is 35%.

In addition, when a "C" corporation distributes profits to the shareholders through dividends, the shareholders pay income taxes on the dividends at a rate of 15%. This results in a double taxation, with an effective maximum tax rate of approximately 44.75%.

To avoid the double taxation, the shareholders of a closely held "C" corporation will "bonus out" the profits of the corporation so that the net profit shown on the corporation's tax return is zero and no corporate taxes are paid. Of course, the bonus, as earned income, is subject to FICA taxes (up to the FICA maximum) and Medicare taxes and income taxes.

The "bonus out" arrangement works only so long as the profit of the corporation is not too large (that is, the bonus is reasonable). If the profit is too large, the IRS will ignore the bonus and treat it as profit, subject to the double tax.

The benefit of "C" status is that the shareholders don't have to pay taxes unless they receive cash from the corporation.

This protects financial partners because they don't have to be concerned with whether the corporation has enough cash to make a distribution at tax time. If they don't get the cash, they don't pay.

If you're expecting outside investment (financial partners), you should plan to be a "C" corporation for tax purposes so the investors do not receive imputed income.

Furthermore, "C" corporation losses can accumulate. Then, when the corporation begins to make profits, it can set off the profits against the past losses and not pay taxes on those amounts.

Appendix D: Business Valuation

Unfortunately, there is no Kelly Blue Book for businesses. And you can't look up recent sales on the Internet, like you can for home sales. But, even if you could, there wouldn't be an easy way to tell whether two businesses are alike or vastly different. So, there'd be no way to compare them.

There are many detailed and intricate methods for valuing a business. But, all business valuations are merely estimates.

Business valuation is part art and part science. Given the same set of circumstances, different appraisers might arrive at different valuations, all for valid reasons.

Any business valuation professional will tell you that a hard and fast valuation figure comes only when there's an actual sale between a willing buyer and seller at arms-length. Only then are all of the factors affecting price (including the financing terms) known.

Business valuation professionals use the financial results of the business, general economic conditions, the business' market information, "soft" variables about the business and prior business sales data, to arrive at an educated guess about a business value. Of course, this takes a fair amount of time and is involved and somewhat expensive.

But, you don't need an expensive, time consuming and "full-blown" valuation to get a reasonable estimate of the value of your business or a target for acquisition.

First, a couple of valuation background items: goodwill and cash flow.

Goodwill.

Goodwill is the name, reputation and relationship between the business and its customers. It's the difference between a going concern business which throws off cash and a bunch of desks, computers and equipment sitting in a storage unit.

Goodwill boils down to providing customers what they want, when and how they want it, easily and at a reasonable price. This creates a relationship between the business and the customers where the customers patronize the business. Sometimes this is referred to as "brand."

You enhance goodwill by focusing on customers and improving their experience and interaction with your business. The goal is make the customer's experience consistent with her highest expectations so she returns to patronize the business again and refers her friends and family.

Many owners think this just means superior products and services or having the lowest price. But being technically competent isn't enough. Nor is it the lowest price. Rather, the human touch is actually more important.

For example, if your accountant does a fantastic job preparing your tax return, finding the most deductions, but doesn't return your calls or files your return late, you won't be satisfied. Yet, if your accountant is personable and has a great relationship with you, you'll tolerate the occasional misstep. And you'll pay a reasonable price.

Doing the job well must go hand-in-hand with a bedside manner.

Customers understand problems can and will happen. If your business is organized so your team can take care of those problems, though, the customer will be satisfied (some say even more than customers who don't have a problem). The difference is the relationship with the customer.

Enterprise Goodwill or Owner Goodwill?

The trick with goodwill in a business purchase, though, is to make sure the goodwill is business (or enterprise) goodwill rather than owner goodwill.

Take my legal practice, for example. People hire me as their lawyer because they know, like and trust me. They don't hire my firm, they hire me. The same often applies to doctors and accountants. This is the owner's personal goodwill and it is very difficult to transfer to a buyer.

Usually, it requires more involvement from the seller and an earn-out arrangement to protect the buyer.

On the other hand, consider for a moment an ice cream store you patronize. Do you patronize that store because of the owner or because of the location or they type of ice cream they serve? I'm guessing its location or type of ice cream. That's an example of business goodwill, which is more easily transferred to a buyer.

Business goodwill is critical to business value because it translates into a consistent, growing and profitable business that generates cash flow. Without it you just have a lease and a bunch of equipment.

Cash Flow.

Business value is tied to cash because cash is the metric for business performance and most buyers are financial buyers. That is, they buy because of the money generated by the business. There must be enough cash flow to pay the buyer's salary and make seller note payments (or provide an investment return if it's an all cash deal). The business must pay for itself and pay you a reasonable salary after a reasonable down payment.

Of course, cash flow is what is left over after all expenses have been paid. Because you'll be the last in line as the business owner, the net cash flow is what you can use to pay your personal expenses and save.

The old saying is absolutely true: cash is king. And cash flow is the business fuel that translates into business value especially in the business sale context. Why? Because when a business is sold the business must pay for itself. In other words, the net cash flow is used by the buyer to purchase the business.

But cash flow in the small business world is very different that cash flow in large businesses.

Large public businesses want as much bottom line profit as possible because their stock price grows with profit. Think P/E (price to earnings) ratio.

On the other hand, independent business owners want to minimize bottom line net profit. Why? Because we all have a silent partner who shows up at the end of each year for his cutoff the till: Uncle Sam. Our government gets a piece of the business bottom line through taxes.

But there is a bit of an "out". The tax laws allow business owners to take deductions for business expenses. And, some of these expenses are "discretionary."

For example, a business owner might take a trip to the annual industry convention in Hawaii, staying at the Hyatt and adding on a couple of days to each end of the trip because of "Jet Lag". The trip is deductible as a business expense. Yet, if she didn't make the trip one year, the business wouldn't suffer.

Or, the owner might have the business pay for his new Mercedes or specialized truck that is used in the business, when an ordinary car or truck would work just as well.

Recasting Financial Statements.

These types of expenses depend on how the owner of the business wants to operate it. But, they're not essential for the operation of the business; they do not have to be incurred in order to generate sales for the business.

For a valuation, though, we want to get back to the true earning and cash flow generating capability of the business. To do this we adjust the financial statements for certain types of expenses and income. Expenses are added back to the net profit of the business and under-paid expenses are deducted from net profit. This process is called "recasting the financial statements" and the end result is the "Seller's Discretionary Earnings or Adjusted Net".

Under-paid expenses would include, for example, an owner's spouse who works in the business but is not paid a salary. Or, the business not paying rent on a building owned by the business owner. The real values of these under-paid expenses are deducted from the net income of the business.

In addition to discretionary expenses and under-paid expenses, an adjustment is also made for anything that is not related to the operation of the business.

These include depreciation and amortization, and non-operating expenses or income. An example of non-operating income would be the sale of a piece of equipment by the business. The income from the sale would be deducted from net profit of the business. For businesses with less than $3MM in annual revenue, the owner's salary expense is also treated as a non-operating expense.

Recasting is done for several years of business operations and the results are averaged using a weighted average.

Market Data Analysis.

Once the recasting is completed, the next step is to compare it with other business sales that have taken place.

The sales data varies based on a number of factors about each business that was sold, including gross sales and adjusted net.

So a mathematical projection is calculated based on comparing the business being valued to the sales data that is closest to that business usually in the areas of gross sales and adjusted net.

Then a trend line for the data – technically called "linear regression" – is calculated to come up a multiple that will be applied to gross sales and adjusted net income to arrive at an estimate of fair market value.

Understanding Multipliers and Return on Investment.

Multipliers are another way of expressing a return on investment from money used to buy the business. A multiplier for a business is a statement of the risk involved in owning and operating that business as compared with the other investments available to a buyer and the time and cost of selling (liquidating) the business.

The higher the multiplier the lower the risk.

For example, a multiplier of 2 means that for each dollar of adjusted net generated by the business, the value of the business is $2.00. A multiplier of 2 also means that a buyer should receive a 50% annual return on her investment in the business. (Multipliers in this range typically include owner salary in the calculation of the annual return on investment.)

Alternatively, a multiplier of 4 means that for each dollar of adjusted net generated by the business, the value of the business is $4.00 and a buyer should receive a 25% annual return on her investment in the business.

In theory, the return on an investment is proportional to the risk.

Take, for example, a "no-risk" investment such as government bonds. If they're generating annual returns of 5%, this means that without any risk at all you could take the money you'll be putting into a small business and earn a 5% annual return on investment ("ROI").

On the other hand, because they are more risky, blue chip stocks traded on a stock exchange must yield a higher average ROI. Historically this is approximately 12% to 14% on average over a long time period. And small public company stock (known as 'small cap stocks'), which are still more risky, yield a higher average ROI of approximately 18% to 22%.

To the financial world and most buyers, owning and operating a small business carries very high risk. Small businesses do not have professional management, ready access to capital or large customer bases, and they can't be sold with a call to your broker. So the ROI is expected to be higher, sometimes much higher, than the returns listed above.

For small business the ROI might be as high as 100%, but more typically between 50% and 25%.

As describe above, the multiplier used for the adjusted cash flow of the business is merely one divided by the ROI. So, an ROI of 50% means the multiplier is 2 and an ROI of 33.33% means the multiplier is 3.

If the business is heavily dependent on the owner (e.g., the goodwill is owner goodwill), the industry is changing, the earnings fluctuating rapidly or there is a lot of competition, the multiplier could be as low as one.

The ROI (and multiplier) are also affected by other "soft" factors, including:

- Overall "health" and performance of the business compared with other similar businesses;
- Cost of entry for new participants;
- Market changes – growing, constant or contracting;
- Competition – severe, moderate or limited;
- Legal Environment – not regulated, regulated or regulation looming;
- Business Assets – new and updated or requiring servicing or replacement;
- Employees – longevity, skill set, restrictive covenant agreements;
- Intellectual Property;
- Facilities;
- Market Image.

Depending on the industry and the size of the business, a multiple for adjusted net or seller's discretionary income could range from 0.5 to 3.5. "Typical" multiples for smaller businesses - those with gross revenues under $1MM, - range from 2 to 2.5 adjusted net.

The actual multiple is established using the database and adjusting for the length of time the business has been in operation and the financial results (owner benefit) compared with the other businesses in the data sample. When cash flow is consistent and growing at a reasonable (but not too high) rate or the business is in an established industry, the multiplier can be a bit higher than the multiplier calculated from the data. There's less risk, so the return on investment can be reduced.

What if there's no cash flow?
When there is no cash flow from a business, there is usually little or no goodwill for the business. In that situation an asset based approach is used to determine the value. This is usually a bottom end price or liquidation value for a business.

The approach is pretty straight forward: the current liquidation market price for each of the business' assets is calculated. Any assets that cannot be liquidated, such as special equipment, or other assets for which there is no market, are ignored.

If the valuation is conducted for the sale of the business in a single transaction where the buyer is expected to restart operations, then special assets, equipment installation expenses and leasehold improvements are included in the asset value.

Debt Service Capability as an Indicator of Value.
As an alternative to the market data method described above, you can back into a price based on the debt that could be serviced with adjusted net less a reasonable salary, after a reasonable down payment.

Using this somewhat unconventional method, the maximum business value is arrived at as follows: (1) a reasonable owner salary is deducted from the adjusted net of the business (this is the "Available Debt Service Payment"; (2) determine the initial principal amount of a loan with a payment in the amount of the result of Available Debt Service Payment (this is the "Acquisition Loan Amount"); and (3) add a reasonable down payment to the Acquisition Loan Amount to determine the selling price.

Obviously there are a few variables that have to be agreed upon to use this method.

Reasonable Salary.

The first of these is a reasonable salary. While you and the seller may differ when it comes to the amount of a reasonable salary, being conservative with the amount is best. A conservative salary would be the lower of what you'd have to pay an employee to do the work or, if you're going to run the business yourself, your living expenses.

Of course, if this is an add-on acquisition and no additional employee time is required to administer the acquired business, you could elect to make this zero. I think that's a mistake, though. The business should stand-alone and the extra benefit to your present business should be gravy. After all, another financial buyer would make the calculation described above.

Another important point: by growing the business, you can increase your compensation or payoff the acquisition loan early. This is why it's very important that you have a strategy to grow the business you're buying.

Acquisition Loan Terms.
Depending on the amount of financing, the term of payments can be between three and seven years and the interest rate from just below to a bit above prime. The term should never be more than ten years.

Reasonable Down Payment.
When it comes to seller financing, a reasonable down payment on a small business is between 40% and 70% of the purchase price. I'd suggest you go with 40% as an initial projection. This means that you'll divide the Acquisition Loan Amount by 0.6 to arrive at the sales price.

Many times, because they've purchased homes, first time buyers think 10% or 20% is appropriate. It isn't. From the seller's perspective, you must have enough skin in the game so you won't walk out if things get difficult.

Putting it Together.
Let's take a simple example.

Say the business generates $125,000 of adjusted net each year. A reasonable salary for you is $50,000 per year. The seller is willing to carry a note for no more than five years at 8% interest with monthly payments of principal and interest fully amortized over the life of the loan (that means they're equal monthly payments without any balloon).

Step 1. Take $125,000 (adjusted net) and deduct $50,000 (reasonable salary). The result, $75,000.00 is the Available Debt Service Payment.

Step 2. The initial principal balance of a loan bearing annual interest of 8% over 60 months with payments of $6,250.00 per month is a bit less than $310,000.00.

Step 3. Assuming a 40% down payment, the business is worth $310,000.00 divided by 0.6, or almost $517,000.00. And the down payment would be $207,000.00.

It's important to remember that this is the maximum value and just a reality check to make sure the other valuation method makes sense. It should be compared to the value to the value arrived through the market data method. The multiple in this example would be 4.13 which would probably be too high for the typical small business.

Of course, you can vary the terms by extending the note, reducing the interest rate or having a balloon payment. But, most sellers would rather have the note payments be made over five years or less to reduce the risk.

Adjustments for Future Cash Requirements.

It's also important to remember that a valuation also assumes that the business does not need a large influx of cash in a short period of time. Many times you'll find sellers who put the business up for sale in the last year of their lease, right before a big increase is expected. Or, the equipment may be worn out and need replacement, or the facility may require an expensive redecoration.

If these or similar situations arise, the monthly cash flow must be adjusted for the additional expense or debt service (and you have to be sure you can get that cash).

About the Author

Ed Alexander helps entrepreneurs start-up, purchase, fund, improve, protect and cash-out (exit) from their businesses. He has represented entrepreneurs and their ventures since he became a lawyer in 1993.

Ed is the founder of the Entrepreneurship Law Firm, P.L., located in Orlando, Florida, and is admitted to practice law in both Florida and New York.

He is also a licensed transaction advisor in Florida and a principal of FitzGibbon Alexander, Inc., a consulting and business transaction advisory firm.

Ed is a member of the Greater Orlando Chamber of Commerce Entrepreneurial Advisory Counsel and the United States Small Business Administration Small Business Resource Network. Ed works closely with University of Central Florida Technology Incubator (UCFTI) client and Seminole County Technology Incubator clients and is regularly requested to present the "Legal and Ethical Foundations" portion of the UCFTI Entrepreneurship Certificate Course.

Ed is author of "*5 Business Killing Mistakes*" and "*The Entrepreneur's No-Nonsense Nuts and Bolts New Venture Legal Guide.*"

Prior to law school, Ed held non-legal positions in the business world with technology companies, including positions with a pacemaker manufacturer, custom integrated circuit manufacturer and laser bar code manufacturer. He has been part of teams that designed software and hardware for the first generation of defibrillator pacemakers, as well as custom analog and digital integrated circuits used in, among other applications, automobiles and hearing aids.

In 1995, Ed was awarded U.S. Patent, No. 5,468,952, for his 1992 invention of a combined miniature high-speed scanner and portable handheld computer.

Ed has been an Adjunct Professor for the University of Central Florida (School of Business) teaching the *New Venture Finance* course in the Entrepreneurship Business Management Concentration, and was 2007 Chairman of the East Orlando Chamber of Commerce.

He works with the Orange County Legal Aid Society as a volunteer guardian ad-litem for abused and neglected children. He also enjoys outdoor activities including fishing, kayaking, hiking, backpacking and hunting.

ENTREPRENEURSHIP LAW FIRM, P.L.
Advising Business Owners

The Entrepreneurship Law Firm is focused on helping entrepreneurs start-up, purchase, improve, protect and cash out from their businesses.

How Entrepreneurship Law Firm is different from other law firms:

Fixed Prices

When you work with Entrepreneurship Law Firm you know what it will cost you BEFORE you get the bill. We believe that once we agree on the work you want done, we should be responsible for the time it takes to do that work. Many law firms, on the other hand, put the risk on you. With those law firms, you never know what your work will cost until you get the bill.

Business Experience

I've been on both sides of the table – businessman and business attorney. This experience provides a unique perspective that many other business attorneys don't have. I truly understand business. I don't try to eliminate all of the risk for you – it can't be done and only serves to kill deals. Rather, I identify the risks and how you may be able to minimize them. Then you make the call about those risks that are acceptable and those that aren't.

Focus on Entrepreneurs

We only work with entrepreneurs and understand the unique challenges you face.

Services:

- Commercial Contracts.
- Shareholder, Operating and Partnership Agreements.
- Business Owner Disputes.
- Commercial and Contract Claims.
- Purchase and Sale Transactions.
- Raising Capital.
- Negotiating Leases.
- Franchise Agreements and Disclosure Documents.
- Independent Contractor Agreements.
- Non-Compete Agreements.
- Employment Contracts.
- Sales Agreements.
- Service Agreements.
- Website Development Agreements.
- Software Development Agreements.
- Strategic Alliances.
- Licensing Technology and Intellectual Property.
- Collecting Accounts Receivable.
- Corporate Documentation.
- Employee Stock Option Plans.
- Employee Restricted Stock Grants.
- Business Workouts and Dissolution.

FitzGibbon Alexander, Inc. is focused on the professional marketing and sale of businesses for business owners and the direct sourcing of solid businesses for buyers.

How FitzGibbon Alexander, Inc. is different:

Business Ownership Experience

As business owners that have participated in purchasing, building, and selling our own businesses, we understand the risks involved in business transactions and can assist our clients in mitigating those risks. Our ownership experience spans a diverse range of industries.

Singular Focus

Our business is selling your business or sourcing an acquisition for you. We don't dabble in residential real estate or other related brokerage business. This way we can design a marketing approach that is effective at either the Private Equity or Main Street level.

Education and Professional Criterion

With the principals holding a law degree, Certified Business Intermediary designation, MBA, Florida Real Estate Brokers license, and many other distinctions between them, they are uniquely qualified to handle the various elements of a business transaction.

Priority Service

While many firms engage as many assignments as possible and hope that one or two sell, FitzGibbon Alexander will only take on a limited number of engagements at a time so that we can prioritize our focus on each engagement. This is especially critical since the data supports the fact that only 1 in 5 businesses listed for sale actually sell.

Services:

- Business Valuation Services
- Marketing and Sale of Businesses
- Guidance on Preparing a Business for Sale
- Direct Sourcing of Add-on Acquisitions to Fuel Growth
- Guidance on Succession Planning Alternatives
- Education on the Buying and Selling Process
- Business Transaction Services
- Guidance on Buying/Selling a Franchise
- Guidance on Maximizing the Value of Your Business

www.FitzgibbonAlexander.com